A Key To The Catholic Pentecostal Renewal

Volume Two

Monsignor Vincent M. Walsh

Key of David Publications
222 N. 17th St.
Philadelphia, Pa. 19103-1299

First Printing – ©1985

Excerpts from the New American Bible © 1970 are used with the permission of the copyright owner—The Confraternity of Christian Doctrine

Library of Congress Catalog Card Number:
ISBN: 0-943374-12-X

© 1985 by Monsignor Vincent M. Walsh
all rights reserved
Key of David Publications
222 N. 17th Street,
Philadelphia, Pa. 19103

Printed in the United States of America

DEDICATION

To those charismatic leaders who have sacrificed so much to keep alive this fire of the New Pentecost in the Church of Philadelphia

TABLE OF CONTENTS

PREFACE

SINCE 1974

The first volume, "A Key to Charismatic Renewal in the Catholic Church," appeared in the Fall of 1974. Since then much has happened.

(1) In the United States, the Renewal's "wild-fire" growth stage has given way to a settling down, with fewer entering and fewer leaving. Although large numbers show a continued interest in the Renewal, most Catholics are totally uninterested.

(2) The renewal is no longer a threat. The Renewal's theology is somewhat to the right. Its practices have not caused Church unrest. Its inability to increase its numbers means that greater future power is not in the wings.

A close observer of the Renewal, even in 1974, would have seen many built-in frailties:

(1) The lack of active priest involvement.

(2) The lack of leaders who could effectively guide large charismatic groups.

(3) The fragility of the prayer group structure.

(4) The inability to provide pastoral care after the initiation of the Baptism of the Spirit.

TWO ASPECTS

Like Jesus Himself, the Renewal has two aspects, the phenomenon and the underlying reality. For Jesus, the phenomenon was the crowd's enthusiasm. The underlying reality was His unity with His Father and His future gift of the Spirit. Jesus never based His claims upon the crowds, often issuing strong disclaimers of their cries to make Him King.

His claim was rooted in His relationship to the Father. His promises centered upon His future gift of the Spirit.

Like Jesus, the Renewal had the phenomenon of crowds but this was never the source of its true claims. The first volume (Question 30, Page 15) gave four reasons for the Renewal's lasting effects, none of which were the crowds. The Renewal's lasting gift rests upon the underlying reality of its theology, powers and practices.

THE PURPOSE OF THIS VOLUME

In beginning this second volume, I sought the Lord's word. What was to be written? The words came, "In the first book you described what was already existing. Now you will describe what will be." Those words have been the constant guiding light of every chapter.

However, the Table of Contents does not immediately reveal a futuristic agenda and even the individual questions do not speak of future events.

What, then, is so futuristic? Why will this power not pass away? Why does the Renewal contain the power to prepare the Church for the Third Millenium? The answers lie in the theology, powers and practices of this Renewal, with their potential only slightly revealed.

THE PHILADELPHIA RENEWAL SINCE 1974

Much has happened personally since Volume One appeared (Fall 1974). Since 1974, the forty Philadelphia prayer groups have grown to over one hundred and sixty. In 1976, my unofficial role in the Philadelphia groups was confirmed by the title of Episcopal Vicar for the Charismatic Prayer Groups.

Besides the prayer groups, other supporting structures have evolved:

1976-   Priest Prayer Dinner (monthly)

1977-   Priest Conference (annual) and formation of Regional Structures.

1978-   Beginning of Key of David Publications and monthly newsletter.

1979-   Vigil of Pentecost celebration; Weekend Conference; Retreat for Sisters; Leadership Conference.

1983-   Charismatic School (Fall and Spring Sessions); Men's Prayer Breakfast.

1984-   Young Adult Prayer Group (monthly)

1985-   Open Mass sponsored by Priest Prayer Group (monthly)

All of the above still flourish and provide the needed support for the prayer group structure.

THE TITLE

Originally, this Renewal was called, the Catholic Pentecostal Movement, or, The Pentecostal Movement in the Catholic Church. In the early 1970's, the name was changed to Charismatic Renewal, the most common term in the United States.

In other countries, the Renewal has many different titles. At the leadership conference in Rome (Spring 1984), Cardinal Suenens asked that the single title, Catholic Pentecostal Renewal, be used everywhere.

In obedience to the Cardinal's wishes, that title has been used for this book. It also provides an easy distinction between the two volumes.

PROLOGUE

This book stresses the power of the Spirit's Pentecostal gifts and asks for a full incorporation of these internal and external manifestations into the Catholic Church.

The advocacy for charisms can obscure the actions of the Spirit in guiding the Catholic Church over the past 2,000 years. Stressing religious experiences can leave the reader with the feeling that the institutional Church is not an important question. Urging a theology of the Spirit can give the impression that a theology of the Church is secondary.

All of these possible misconceptions led to this a prologue and a clear statement about the Catholic Church.

Concerning the Church, I believe that:

1) Jesus deliberately chose those followers to whom He would appear in Easter visions and upon whom He would first send His Spirit.

2) These followers went forth from Jerusalem and founded churches which were united to each other through Apostolic Sees.

3) These apostles exercised the full authority needed to keep these churches united in faith and morals.

4) These founding apostles saw the need for continued Church authority after they were gone. They provided for the conferal of office by the laying on of hands.

5) The Catholic Church can rightly trace its historical roots back to those same apostles.

6) Over the next six centuries, the Spirit guided the Church to delineate the Apostles Creed, the canon of Scripture, and the basic doctrines of Christianity.

7) Even though the Spirit acts everywhere, many of His charisms are present only in the Catholic Church. These include indefectibility (lasting until the end of time), infallibility (the faithful guidance of the Spirit in teaching doctrine and morals), apostolicity (going back to apostolic times) and universality (spread throughout the world).

8) The Catholic Church has especially the charism of unity and will be the unique instrument of the Spirit in bringing about the unity of Christendom, and the unity of Christianity and Israel.

Over the past five years, I have become immersed in the Church Fathers, Church History, and the historical development of dogmas. Such reading forcefully recalls how powerfully the Spirit has guided the Church.

In these past twenty centuries, people and nations have often declared the Church dead and have said there would be no more popes (as when Pius VI was persecuted by Napoleon and died in a French jail in August, 1799). Contrast that dilemma with today, when every public action and word of Pope John Paul II is videotaped by the secular media.

May my strong advocacy for Pentecostal gifts never obscure the Spirit's special 2,000 year guidance of the Catholic Church.

Section One
Basic Elements

Chapter 1
SENDING THE SPIRIT

On many occasions, Jesus promised to send His Spirit (Lk 24:49; Jn 14:26; Jn 15:26; Jn 16:7; Acts 1:8). However, because Catholics know that the Spirit is God and that God is everywhere, "sending the Spirit" seems to be just a clever metaphor.

History, also, takes its toll. The original sending brought forth "signs and wonders". Then everything went back to normal so to speak, (as if Church life without God's powerful interventions can in any way be called normal). Jesus' "sending the Spirit" gradually lost all meaning. St. Thomas Aquinas does not even devote a question to Jesus' sending the Spirit. (Summa Theologica, Book Three) He lists Jesus' last act as sitting at the right hand of the Father.

Even a Pentecostal Renewal can get lost, thinking that its focus is charisms and personal experiences while forgetting that the primary gift is the Spirit Himself.

The Early Church claimed it was the New Israel. Paul claimed that Christians, not Jews, were the true children of Abraham. These fantastic, self-proclaimed privileges and assumptions were based on the sending of the Spirit which

1

ushered in the Final Age. Before rushing ahead into Pentecostal Renewal's many truths and practices, this chapter makes clear that the great moment in human history occurred when Jesus "delivered over His Spirit" (Jn 19:30).

A) UNDERSTANDING THE SENDING

1) *Since the Spirit is God and already present everywhere, how can He be sent?*

Jesus didn't send the Spirit in the way that a parent sends a child on an errand. Also, this "sending" did not mark the beginning of the Spirit's work (He was already active in the Old Testament).

This "sending" marked a change in the relationship of mankind to God, just as the Father's sending of Jesus began a new relationship.

2) *How can God enter into a new relationship with mankind?*

Scripture records three new relationships:

- a) God revealing Himself in the Old Testament
- b) God becoming a man in Jesus
- c) God sending His Spirit

3) *Did the Father or Jesus send the Spirit?*

Scripture correctly says that both sent the Spirit.

1) "…the Paraclete, the Holy Spirit
whom the Father will send in my name,…"
(Jn 14:26)

2) "when the Paraclete comes,
   the Spirit of truth who comes from the Father—
   and whom I myself will send from the Father—
   ..." (Jn 15:26)

For ease of expression, this chapter will speak of Jesus sending the Spirit.

4) What does "sending the Spirit" mean?

It means, basically, two things:

1) The Spirit is now a universal gift, available to all.

2) His powers within each person are beyond any previous scope.

5) Wasn't the Spirit always available to everyone?

In theory, anyone could receive and experience the Spirit. However, even among the Chosen People, experiencing the Spirit was not universal. An example might help. In theory, every human being can read. However, without universal education, most never experience this gift. Schools make education closer and more available, just as Jesus' sending made the Spirit closer and more available.

6) How are His powers within the believer beyond any previous scope?

The Spirit enjoys two sets of powers, sanctifying and charismatic. Sanctification means uniting the person to God. Charismatic means equipping the person for ministry to others.

3

Jesus, of course, was uniquely united to God and exercised an unheard of charismatic ministry. In both areas, He was beyond any previous relationship of man to God. Jesus' gift of the Spirit offers to all believers a personal sharing in His own sanctifying and charismatic powers.

B) VARIOUS SENDINGS

7) *When was the Spirit sent?*

Since the New Testament contains various streams of the Christian experience, the exact moment cannot be pinpointed. Luke (Acts 2:4) pictures the Spirit being sent at Pentecost. John (20:22) pictures Jesus bestowing the Spirit on Easter Sunday evening.

Clearly, the Spirit was sent after Jesus' death and resurrection. John even speaks of there being no Spirit before the Resurrection. "Here, he was referring to the Spirit, whom those that came to believe in him, were to receive. There was, of course, no Spirit as yet, since Jesus had not yet been glorified." (7:39)

8) *Why could the Spirit only be sent after the death and glorification of Jesus?*

Sending the Spirit is Jesus' prerogative as Lord. Therefore, this sending could only take place after Jesus entered into His glory. Peter explained that sequence in his Pentecost sermon: "Exalted at God's right hand, he first received the promised Holy Spirit from the Father, then poured this Spirit out on us." (Acts 2:33)

9) Are there various types of sendings?

There is Jesus' universal sending, which means the Spirit assumes a new, more available relationship to all people and there are the individual sendings into each person's life.

10) What is the difference between Jesus' sending His Spirit and the individual sendings into each person's heart?

Jesus' sending of the Spirit marked the final age and means that the Spirit now stands in a new and definitive relationship to mankind. The individual sendings are the believer's receiving, taking advantage of, and profiting from Jesus' sending.

11) Are there various individual sendings?

Since the Spirit is often "sent" to each person, there are a variety of sendings. Some of these sendings are meant for all and some are very personal, unique to the individual.

12) What is an example of each?

The sending of personal justification, whereby the person becomes a child of God, is meant for all.

Other sendings, such as a call to be a martyr, to prophesy, or to heal, serve particular needs and are not for all.

C) MEANS OF SENDING THE SPIRIT

13) In individual cases is the Spirit sent directly or through others?

The Acts show both types of sendings. Sometimes God acted directly, as in the Pentecost scene (2:1-4), and also in the house gathering after Peter and John were released from prison:

> "The place where they were gathered shook as they prayed. They were filled with the Holy Spirit and continued to speak God's word with confidence." (4:31)

At other times, the Spirit is sent by means of preaching, belief and the laying on of hands.

14) Which is the more usual way?

Usually, the Spirit is sent through others. In the Early Church, this became the somewhat normal procedure. As this happened more often, it became seen as a regularly expected result. From their personal missionary experiences, the disciples came to some important conclusions.

1) They themselves had the unique experiences of seeing the Risen Jesus and of receiving the Spirit directly.

2) This direct receiving of the Spirit could happen anytime.

3) However, there was no need to depend on these unique special actions of God.

4) If people believed the apostolic preaching, they would receive the Spirit through Baptism and the laying on of hands.

5) People did not have to see the mortal or risen Jesus to receive the Spirit. They only had to hear and believe in the story of Jesus.

D) IMPORTANCE OF BELIEF IN THE SENDING

15) *Why is it important to believe that Jesus sent His Spirit?*

For the same reason it is important to believe in Baptism or Eucharist. Without belief, the gift is set aside.

16) *Why is belief in Jesus sending the Spirit as important as belief in Baptism and Eucharist?*

Jesus sending His Spirit is the primary mystery. The Spirit is His first gift. All the other mysteries and gifts flow from the Spirit's being sent.

17) *How do all the other gifts flow from the Spirit?*

All of God's gifts to the Church come from the Spirit. The Spirit is the soul of the Church. Every power in the Church comes from the Spirit, whom Jesus sent.

As Catholics, we are called to believe in sacraments, the inspiration of Scripture, the indefectibility and infallibility of the Church, and many other truths. All of these come from the Holy Spirit.

18) *Did Jesus see the sending of the Spirit as important?*

Jesus saw that His entire purpose was to send the Spirit.

"Yet I tell you the sober truth:
It is much better for you that I go.
If I fail to go,
the Paraclete will never come to you,
whereas if I go,
I will send him to you." (Jn 16:7)

19) Why did Jesus see this Sending as so important?

Jesus realized:

1) He had a unique relationship to the Father.

   "The Father and I are one." (Jn 10:30)

2) He was meant to communicate this relationship to all mankind.

   "On that day you will know
   that I am in my Father,
   and you in me, and I in you." (Jn 14:20)

3) This gift would result from His sending the Spirit.

   "The Spirit himself gives witness with our spirit that we are children of God." (Rom. 8:16)

   John takes up that same truth in his first letter:

   "See what love the Father has bestowed on us in letting us be called children of God!
   Yet that is what we are." (3:1)

20) What effects did Jesus foresee?

He knew three things would happen to His disciples by the Spirit's coming:

1) They would share in His own prayer life.

2) They would be totally and deeply changed.

3) They would be ready to witness to the whole world.

E) THE SPIRIT'S EFFECTS UPON THE APOSTLES

21) *What were apostles like before the sending of the Spirit?*

Before the sending, they made little spiritual progress. Concerning prayer, they learned the Our Father but couldn't stay awake in the garden. Concerning the Kingdom, they could only understand a political overthrow of the Romans. Concerning morality, they could not even grasp the idea of a lifelong commitment to marriage. Concerning the cross, they thought that was foolish. Concerning doctrine, they didn't even grasp Jesus' oneness with His Father.

The gospel pictures them as men of good will, but as yet untouched by the Spirit. They were held together only by the mortal human presence of Jesus, Who soon would be removed from them.

22) *What happened to the Apostles?*

The New Testament after Pentecost is a witness to the total change that came over the Apostles from their receiving the Spirit.

F) THE SPIRIT IN THE OLD TESTAMENT

23) *What is the Old Testament picture of the Spirit?*

The Spirit is used in the Old Testament:

1) To solve the doctrinal problem of how a transcendent God (far above all creation) could act upon the world. He did this through His Spirit.

2) To denote God's special blessing and power in the anointed leaders of Israel.

24) *Wasn't the Spirit available to everyone in the Old Testament?*

The picture given in the Old Testament limits the Spirit's actions to a few. The great leaders and prophets are marked with the Spirit, but His activity is never promised nor bestowed on everyone.

25) *What are the outstanding examples of the Spirit being sent in the Old Testament?*

Besides a number of lesser known figures, the following are clearly seen as receiving the Spirit:

1) Joseph (Gen. 41:37)

2) Moses (Num. 11:17)

3) Seventy Elders (Num. 11:26)

4) Saul (1 Sam. 10:16)

5) David (1 Sam. 16:13)

26) Does the Old Testament list any others who receive and experience the Spirit?

Although the Holy Spirit is not directly mentioned, His activity is manifest in the recounted conversion experiences of the prophets, such as:

1) Isaiah (Chap. 6)

2) Jeremiah (Chap. 1)

3) Ezekiel (Chap. 2)

27) Why was the Spirit not sent to everyone in the Old Testament?

The universal gift of the Spirit was a prerogative reserved to Jesus as Lord and would mark the Final Age. Two prophets are important in foreseeing this future event.

1) Joel writes:

> "Then afterward I will pour out
>   my spirit upon all mankind.
> Your sons and daughters shall prophesy,
>   your old men shall dream dreams,
>   your young men shall see visions;...(3:1)"

2) Jeremiah writes:

> "No longer will they have need to teach their friends and kinsmen how to know the Lord. All, from least to greatest, shall know me says the Lord ..." (31:34)

Jeremiah 31:31 is the only place in the Old Testament that uses the phrase "new covenant". The meaning is obvious. In the New Covenant, through a wonderful divine intervention, intermediaries like Moses or the prophets would be unnecessary. (cf. Jerome Biblical Commentary – Chapter 19)

G) THE SPIRIT IN THE NEW TESTAMENT

28) What is the New Testament relationship of Jesus and the Spirit?

The picture is clear:

1) His own union with the Spirit is from the very beginning. (John Chap. 1)

2) His human relationship to the Spirit is from the very beginning of His earthly life. (Mt. Chap. 1 and Luke Chap. 1)

3) His public ministry begins after a special anointing of the Spirit. (Mt. 3:16; Mk 1:10; Lk 3:22; Jn 1:32)

4) He promises the Spirit. (Jn Chaps. 14-16 and Acts Chap. 1)

5) He bestows the Spirit. (Jn 20; 22 and Acts Chap. 2)

29) What role did Jesus' death play in His sending the Spirit?

John cleverly writes, "Then he bowed his head, and delivered over his Spirit" (19:30). The oblation of Jesus' human nature released His Spirit, just as the tearing open of an envelope makes the inner contents available to all.

Paul calls this God's hidden mystery. "None of the rulers of this age knew the mystery; if they had known it, they would never have crucified the Lord of glory." (1 Cor 2:8) In crucifying Jesus, these "rulers" allowed His humanity to become the instrument of sending the Spirit.

30) What is the witness of Paul?

Throughout his writings, Paul constantly fights against Judaizers who want people to practice the Old Law. Paul argues against this returning to the Law because:

1) The Law couldn't send the Spirit.

2) Restoring the Law would make void the mystery of Jesus, Who alone is the source of the Spirit.

31) What Scripture texts highlight this vision of Paul?

The following texts bring out Paul's understanding:

1) Powerlessness of the Old Law.

> "The Law was powerless because of its weakening by the flesh." (Rom 8:3)

2) Inability of the Law to bestow the Spirit:

> "I want to learn only one thing from you; how did you receive the Spirit? Was it through observance of the law or though faith in what you heard?" (Gal 3:2)

3)   The power of faith in Jesus to bestow the Spirit:

> "Is it because you observe the law or because you have faith in what you heard, that God lavishes the Spirit on you and works wonders in your midst?" (Gal 3:5)

4)   Continued belief in law would negate Christ's gift.

> "Pay close attention to me, Paul, when I tell you that if you have yourselves circumcised, Christ will be of no use to you!" (Gal 5:2)

H)   PRAYER TONGUES AND THE SENDING

32)   Did Jesus give any special external sign to His sending the Spirit?

The sign of the Spirit's sending is the manifestation of prayer in tongues.

> "All were filled with the Holy Spirit. They began to express themselves in foreign tongues and make bold proclamation, as the Spirit prompted them." (Acts 2:4)

33)   Wasn't this a "one-time" extraordinary sign to convince the disciples?

The manifestation of prayer tongues is recorded in two other important sendings of the Spirit.

First, the conversion and Baptism of the Gentiles depended on this clear sign of praying in tongues:

"The circumcised believers who had accompanied Peter were surprised that the gift of the Holy Spirit should have been poured out on the Gentiles also, whom they could hear speaking in tongues and glorifying God." (Acts 10:45-46)

Secondly, the unique power of Jesus' Baptism is highlighted at Ephesus as Paul baptizes and lays hands on John's disciples:

"When they heard this, they were baptized in the name of the Lord Jesus. As Paul laid his hands on them, the Holy Spirit came down on them and they began to speak in tongues and to utter prophecies." (Acts 19:5-6)

The Acts, therefore, makes prayer in tongues a clear sign that Jesus' Spirit has been sent.

34) Why is prayer in tongues such a scriptural sign?

For two reasons:

1) Prayer in tongues is the only manifestation of the Spirit that is not recorded before Pentecost. In God's design, this gift was withheld to show that Jesus' sending the Spirit is truly a new gift.

2) In both the conversion of the Gentiles and of John's disciples, prayer in tongues is a clear, external sign, easily and quickly discerned by all.

35) Is the Spirit sent to those who don't pray in tongues?

The Spirit has many manifestations. In the three examples of prayer tongues in Acts, the people involved also proclaimed God's wonders. This is a further sign of receiving the Spirit.

36) If the Spirit has many manifestations and is received by those not praying in tongues, what is the importance of tongues?

If praying in tongues is set aside, the importance of Jesus sending His Spirit is also downgraded. The two are inevitably linked. If people are interested in the Spirit, they also must be interested in prayer tongues. The two go together.

37) What happens if tongues are set aside and the Spirit's sending is downgraded?

To some degree, God's people revert back to the powerlessness of the Old Testament Law, and many problems reassert themselves. These problems include:

1) believers who have no personal experience of Jesus.

2) a growing power of sinfulness, both individual and collective, unchecked by the Spirit's power.

3) a loss of Christian identity, both in the believer and in the Church.

I) WHY OVERLOOKED?

38) *Is the sending of the Spirit seen as an important mystery?*

Even though the Spirit's sending is as great a mystery as the sending of Jesus, it is often overlooked as unimportant.

39) *Is there any reason for overlooking this mystery?*

Because Jesus assumed a human nature and lived an historical life, Christians have tended to focus on the Father's sending Jesus. Because Jesus' rising from the dead was so extraordinary, Christians have seen the Resurrection as a mystery proving Jesus' claims. Therefore, Christian belief tends to see Jesus' work as consisting of His becoming man, dying on the cross, rising from the dead, and sitting at the Father's right hand.

40) *Why do believers overlook this mystery of the Spirit?*

For one reason, the Spirit was already active. He acted in the Old Testament, especially in the prophets. He was also active in Jesus' life and ministry. Therefore, Jesus sending His Spirit is often dismissed as unimportant because the Spirit is not entirely new to the Scriptural story.

41) *What will happen if the Church once more sees the Spirit's sending as important?*

Church life will recapture its true foundation. Peter's Pentecost sermon summarizes the basic missionary preaching, used constantly by the Early Church. That preaching stressed that:

1) Jesus received the promised Spirit.

2) He poured out the Spirit on all.

3) That Spirit is available to all who believe. (Acts 2:14-41)

This book tries to describe a church renewed by a strong belief in the Sending of the Spirit.

Chapter 2
THE APOSTOLIC EXPERIENCE

The Apostolic Community was unique, the human recipient of Jesus' gift of the Spirit. Since the Catholic Church only has what that community passed on, it·is important to grasp what they received. We have received from them the Apostolic Tradition. However, is that all they received and all they passed on? The Catholic Church rightly speaks about the "deposit of faith", those Christian truths about God and about life usually called "faith and morals". Catholics believe that the Pope cannot err in matters of faith and morals because His role is to preserve that deposit of faith. However, is faith and morals the only gifts passed on?

Before the Apostolic Tradition was there not an Apostolic Experience? Even a quick New Testament reading shows clearly that the apostles enjoyed an experience of the Risen Jesus and of His Holy Spirit. In the next decades, the Apostolic Community was formed by these ongoing experiences of the Spirit. In light of their experiences that community formulated the doctrinal truths and the models of Christian living. Obviously, the Apostolic Experience preceded and formed the Apostolic Tradition.

Because experiences are personal, they are usually limited to those who receive them. However, the Apostolic Experience comes from the Spirit who is available to all.

This book focuses on personal religious experiences. This chapter deliberately recalls that the Apostolic Experience preceded and formed the Tradition. People should know that the Apostolic Experience is also supposed to be their experience.

(A) UNDERSTANDING THE APOSTOLIC EXPERIENCE

1) *What is the Apostolic Experience?*

It is the Apostolic Community's receiving and cooperating with the Spirit's sending. This experience manifests the Spirit's new relationship to every human being.

2) *What is this new relationship?*

When the Second Person of the Trinity became flesh, He entered into a new relationship with mankind. When the Spirit was sent, He, too, entered into a new relationship (the entire thrust of the previous chapter). The Spirit, however, was not personally united to one human nature, but was sent to all humanity. The Apostolic Experience is the manifestation of the Spirit's new relationship to every human being.

3) Is this Experience personal or communal?

Both. Every member of the Apostolic Community personally experienced the Spirit. However, these experiences were strongly communal. Most received the Spirit while joined together with others. (The disciples in the Upper Room; the women going to the tomb; the two Emmaus disciples). If received alone, the person always shared with or validated the gift through the community.

4) Wasn't Paul's experience on the road to Damascus totally personal?

Not at all. The gift was completed only as Ananias laid hands on him. (Acts 9:17) Also, Paul himself later confirmed the validity of his experiences by conferring with the other apostles. (Gal. 2:6)

5) Why was this Experience always communal?

Because this Experience is an important part of the Church's foundation, it had to be communal. Christianity cannot be based upon just one person's experiencing of the Spirit. Scripture records that the disciples used one another to confirm the validity of their personal experiences.

(B) RELATIONSHIP TO THE SENDING

6) What is the relationship of the Apostolic Experience to the Sending of the Spirit?

This Experience is the first result of the Sending and the first personal sign that the gift was given.

7) *Is the Apostolic Experience the full effect of the Sending of the Spirit?*

The Apostolic Experience is only one effect of the Spirit's Sending. Many other gifts, such as the Apostolic Tradition, the sacraments, and Church structure, also came from the Spirit.

Although only one of the Spirit's many gifts, this Apostolic Experience is important and should be highlighted.

8) *Won't this highlighting reduce the Sending of the Spirit to just religious experiences?*

Just the opposite. All experiences have some cause. Overlooking the Apostolic Experience causes us to lose sight of the Spirit's Sending.

(C) RELATIONSHIP TO THE CHURCH

9) *How is the Apostolic Experience related to the other aspects of Church life?*

Besides this Experience, Christianity contains sacraments, creed, and moral standards. All are gifts from the Spirit's Sending. Restoring the Apostolic Experience will not overturn these other Church elements but will effect their renewal.

10) *What is meant by "restoring the Apostolic Experience"?*

The Church teaches that the Apostles believed in certain truths, administered sacraments, and taught certain moral standards. This chapter highlights that, besides those three activities, they also experienced the Spirit, both individually and communally.

Restoring the Apostolic Experience means the Church not only teaches the creed, sacraments, and moral law handed down by the Apostles, but also preaches the Experience of the Spirit enjoyed by them.

11) Can the present Church enjoy the same religious experiences that the Apostles had?

Usually, experiences are personal and cannot be communicated. However, these religious experiences came from the Spirit, and are supposed to be available until the end of time.

12) Is the Apostolic Experience the same as the Baptism of the Spirit?

The two are not the same. "To baptize in the Spirit" (Mt 3:11; Mk 1:8, 3:16; Jn 1:33) and "to be baptized in the Spirit" (Acts 1:5 and 11:16) means all of the effects of the Spirit's Sending, not just the Apostolic Experience.

13) How would the Apostolic Experience differ from our own religious experience?

Two parts of the Apostolic Experience are unique to those who received the gift:

1) The way the Apostolic Community received the gift.

2) The privilege of being the model for future believers.

However, these aspects of uniqueness don't mean that the content of the Experience is limited to the original group.

14) What is the content of the Apostolic Experience?

The content includes all the ways the disciples were touched by the Spirit. This included:

1) The power to pray as Jesus prayed.

2) The sense of oneness with the Father.

3) The ability to yield to the Spirit's charisms.

4) The help to live up to Christ's preaching.

15) Did they believe that this Experience was unique to them?

The way they received the gift was unique. They knew that others would not see the human Jesus or experience the Easter visions. However, they also knew from the events after Pentecost, that the Apostolic Experience was not limited to the original Apostolic Community.

16) How did others enter into the Apostolic Experience?

Those coming later, including the Gentiles, received the gift by having faith in the gospel message and by being baptized.

> "My message and my preaching had none of the persuasive force of 'wise' argumentation but the convincing power of the Spirit." (1 Cor. 2:4)

Since the Spirit was the source of their own experiences, the apostles believed the Spirit was the source of everyone's conversion.

17) How is the Experience related to the Trinity?

Every valid Christian experience always touches upon all three Divine Persons. This Apostolic gift came from the Spirit, helped the Early Church to confess that Jesus is Lord, and led them to understand God as Father.

(D) NEW BUT IMPORTANT

18) Why focus on the Apostolic Experience?

The Church always preserves. True renewal means rediscovering all the gifts in the Apostolic Church since these are normative in the Church. Focusing on this Experience recaptures the power of the Early Church.

19) What does "normative" mean?

In the Catholic Church, "normative" means three things:

1) available to all.

2) a regular part of Church life.

3) preached so all believers receive. For example, the Eucharist is a normative gift in the church.

20) Is not the Term "Apostolic Experience" a new term?

Yes. It is deliberately used to try to express a rediscovery of a forgotten aspect.

21) *Is this rediscovery important?*

Everything at the heart and the beginning of Christianity is extremely important. Seeing this Experience as the first gift of the Spirit's Sending, followed later by the Apostolic Tradition, provides a more complete picture of the Spirit's gift.

22) *What results from this rediscovery?*

This rediscovery opens up two understandings:

1) The importance of the conversion experience.

2) The role of religious experiences in daily Catholic life.

23) *What is presently seen concerning religious experiences?*

Currently, religious experiences are seen as "extras", available to those who might seek them. They are not considered truly essential to Christian life. A renewed emphasis on the Apostolic Experience provides a foundation to restore religious experiences to today's Church.

(E) RECEIVING THE APOSTOLIC EXPERIENCE

(Since the Apostolic Experience is the receiving of the Spirit's gift, these questions examine the receiving itself.)

24) *Did anyone perfectly receive the Spirit?*

Mary, according to her human capacity, perfectly received the Spirit, and is extremely important in any understanding of the Apostolic Experience.

25) *How about the other members of the Early Church?*

Their cooperation was limited and flawed. Nevertheless, because their receiving the Spirit was a foundation for future generations, we should believe that their cooperation was sufficient to safeguard the gift.

26) *Is the New Testament, then, imperfect?*

God uses the human instrument in all its imperfection. He doesn't need a perfect Apostolic Church or a perfect New Testament to gain His goal of bringing all into an experience of Jesus.

The imperfect cooperation of the Apostles with the sending of the Spirit still provides an adequate base for all to understand the gift.

(F) SCRIPTURAL BASIS

27) *When did the Apostles begin to receive this gift?*

Since this is a "Christ Experience", they began to receive it from the first moment they met Jesus. However, until the Passion and Resurrection, the Experience remained superficial.

With the Easter visions and Pentecost, this gift deepened and continued for the rest of their lives. Jesus promised this continuing Experience.

> "the Paraclete, the Holy Spirit
> whom the Father will send in my name,
> will instruct you in everything,
> and remind you of all that I told you."
> (Jn 14:26)

28) What Easter visions highlight this "Christ Experience"?

Some Easter visions are simply narrations of Jesus' appearing. Others highlight the personal changes due to the Experience:

1) "They said to one another, 'Were not our hearts burning inside us as he talked to us on the road and explained the Scripture to us?" (Lk 24:32)

2) "They were still incredulous for sheer joy and wonder." (Lk 24:41)

3) "At the sight of the Lord the disciples rejoiced." (Jn 20:20)

4) "Thomas said in response, 'My Lord and my God?" (Jn 20:28)

29) Does Jesus ever describe the Apostolic Experience?

He describes the following effects in His last discourse (Jn C14-17). The Apostles will:

1) Know Jesus' relationship to the Father:
"On that day you will know

that I am in my Father,
and you in me, and I in you."
(14:20)

2)   Know Jesus by divine revelation:
     "I too will love him
     and reveal myself to him." (14:21)

3)   Enjoy a new relationship:
     "Instead, I call you friends,
     since I have made known to you all
       that I heard from my Father." (15:15)

4)   Experience Jesus' Indwelling:
     "To them I have revealed your name,
     and I will continue to reveal it
     so that your love for me may live in
       them,
     and I may live in them." (17:26)

30)   What scriptural texts show that the apostles believed the Apostolic Experience was for others?

The texts are clear.

1)   Peter concluded his Pentecost speech with a
     promise:
       "..then you will receive the gift of
       the Holy Spirit." (Acts 2:38)

2) Peter described the Gentile conversion experience as "the same gift":

"If God was giving them the same gift he gave us when we first believed in the Lord Jesus Christ, who was I to interfere with him?" (Acts 11:17)

3) Paul's question to the Ephesian disciples shows his belief that the Spirit is given at Christian initiation:

"Did you receive the Holy Spirit when you became believers?" (Acts 19:2)

4) Paul writes about the Spirit's internal activity:

"The Spirit himself gives witness with our spirit that we are children of God." (Rom 8:16)

5) Paul expects these experiences to actually prove divine adoption:

"The proof that you are sons is the fact that God has sent forth into our hearts the spirit of his Son which cries out 'Abba!' ('Father!')" (Gal 4:6)

31) What resulted from the Apostolic Experience?

Scripture shows that from these experiences, the Apostolic Church:

1) realized that Jesus was Lord. (Ph 6:2:11)

2) lived a high moral standard. (Eph C5; Cul C3)

3) were drawn together into community. (Acts 4:32)

4) overcame threats and persecutions. (2 Thes 1:4)

5) witnessed to the whole world. (Acts 13:32)

(G) HIGHLIGHTING THE APOSTOLIC EXPERIENCE

32) What is the value of highlighting the Apostolic Experience?

Since the Early Church was formed by the Apostolic Experience, a full appreciation of their Experience will begin an age when all the baptized enjoy the same experiences.

33) Are there any scriptural proofs that these experiences were communicated to the baptized?

Paul often writes in a communal vein, describing experiences that both he and his followers received. He believes his own experiences should be shared by his converts.

"All of us have been given to drink of the one Spirit." (1 Cor 12:13)

34) What proof is there that experiences were involved in the baptism of new believers?

The Letter to the Hebrews describes the baptismal experiences of converts:

"For when men have once been enlightened and have tasted the heavenly gift and become sharers in the Holy Spirit, when they have tasted the good word of God and the powers of the age to come..." (6:4-5)

35) *What is the main purpose of this Chapter?*

This chapter highlights:

1) The importance of the Apostles' religious experiences.

2) The Apostolic belief that new converts should enjoy these same experiences.

A belief in the Apostolic Experience would lead to the conclusion that religious experiences are a normal gift of Baptism. The pastoral conclusions of that belief are enormous.

Chapter 3
THE CONVERSION EXPERIENCE

Pentecostal Renewal does not claim a monopoly on the Spirit's actions. Just the opposite. The Renewal seeks a process whereby what is now in the Renewal's hands will be taken over by the Church.

One of the Renewal's gifts is the ability to bring people to the "Conversion Experience". When people say how much they "got out of the Renewal" or how "they were touched or changed", they are describing in their own words the Conversion Experience. Without this beginning gift, Catholics remain dependent on spiritual food from without. They do not know how to "taste and see" for themselves.

Unfortunately, this Conversion Experience has not penetrated the whole Church. The gift itself, the faith needed, and the necessary pastoral care that can bring it about are generally unknown. Priests don't see themselves as trying to bring their parishioners to any Conversion Experience. It is not a concrete goal in parish preaching.

The purpose of this chapter is to transplant the Conversion Experience gift from the Pentecostal Renewal to the whole Church. The questions focus on parish, Church activity and the vision of a Church that believes in the Conversion Experience.

But be careful. The Conversion Experience is but the first step on a road into the full mystery of God's will. It is an awesome step to fall into the hands of the living God.

"Awful indeed is the Lord's majesty, and wonderful is his power." (Sir 43:30)

(A) UNDERSTANDING THIS GIFT

1) What is the Conversion Experience?

It is God manifesting to the person His divine presence. Being an experience, various signs accompany this gift.

2) What are these signs?

They vary with the person's background and condition, human and spiritual. Some signs include:

1) Tears of joy.

2) Repentance over the past.

3) Peace.

4) A sense of God's presence.

5) Great inner consolation.

6) Personal appreciation of religious doctrines.

There is usually a period of great consolation in prayer which comes fairly quickly. Also, the person finds himself thrust into a spiritual world.

3) What are the effects of this experience?

These are multiple. The person

1) sees areas of his/her life that must change.

2) accepts a new direction for his/her life.

3) receives power for self-discipline.

4) is motivated to go beyond his/her present religious practices.

4) To whom does this happen?

This gift is freely bestowed upon all classes of people. In our time, this experience is happening with greater frequency than ever before. Because of this, the Pentecostal Renewal openly speaks of this experience as universal and available to all.

(B) COMPARISON WITH OTHER EXPERIENCES

5) How does the Conversion Experience differ from other religious experiences?

It differs from prior experiences in the profound changes and new direction of life which follow. The Conversion Experience represents a permanent gift (if cooperated with) and the beginning of an entire life of religious experiences.

It differs from subsequent religious experiences just as a door differs from the rest of the house. The door is the only entrance. The Conversion Experience is the only way to enter a life of experiencing God.

6) What, then, is unique about the Conversion Experience?

It is profound and life-changing. Its effects are meant to remain and become the foundation for all of God's future gifts.

Also, the experience changes the person's direction in life. Even good people realize that this experience invites them to a new level of sharing God's life.

7) Don't many people have profound experiences of God and experience no permanent effects?

Unfortunately, yes. These experiences pass away because people are not taught the importance of these gifts. They are not encouraged to follow through. These experiences are not confirmed as valid. The original Conversion Experience can easily die out if the pastoral helps are not available.

8) How does the Conversion Experience differ from the Baptism in the Spirit?

A true Baptism in the Spirit is the Conversion Experience. However, often the full effects described here are not present in someone who has been prayed over for the Baptism in the Spirit.

9)   *If that is so, then what is lacking?*

The Conversion Experience is God's gift at a very special moment. Sometimes, the person is not yet ready for a complete conversion, or doesn't as yet grasp the degree of God's call.

Frequently, the Baptism of the Spirit through the laying on of hands prepares a person for the later gift of conversion.

(C)   FOSTERING THE GIFT

10)   *What brings about the Conversion Experience?*

This is totally a gift from God, given to the person at a very special moment or period of life. Therefore, nothing human can bring about this experience. However, much can be done to foster this gift.

11)   *What is meant by "fostering"?*

Fostering means making efforts so that something will happen. Fostering this gift means creating the atmosphere and providing the helps so that God can bestow the Conversion Experience. If this is faithfully done, God will bring people to conversion.

12)   *What is needed to foster this experience on a widespread scale?*

Those exercising authority should:

   1)   believe in the gift as a primary step in pastoral care.

2) understand and use those means that allow God to act.

3) develop the pastoral care so that this conversion gift does not die out, nor is seen as a passing phenomenon.

(D) PASTORAL CARE

13) *What is meant by "a primary step in pastoral care"?*

A primary step means the very first goal. It means the foundational beginning for all else that should follow. It means getting to the heart of the matter before moving on to secondary questions.

14) *What means are available to bring about this primary step?*

The first means is very personal. Those serving the Church must themselves have received the Conversion Experience. This beginning gift must still be powerful and alive within them.

Secondly, their teaching and preaching should be filled with stories of people experiencing God and being converted to Him. That makes the Conversion Experience seem real and possible for everyone.

15) *What means should be used to foster the Conversion Experience?*

People who have undergone the Conversion Experience and try to bring this about in others, will develop a variety of means. The primary means will be the Catholic community which they are serving.

This community, itself converted to the Lord, is the usual means for individual Conversion Experiences.

16) ***Why is pastoral care necessary so the Conversion Experience remains effective?***

It is needed because conversion experiences, like the seed in the gospel story, encounter many obstacles to full growth. These seeds fail to mature due to problems, pleasures, anxieties and lack of soil. Careful pastoring is necessary until the final harvest. Without this follow-up help, conversion experiences will occur frequently but will be quickly passing.

17) ***Doesn't this vision of the Conversion Experience see Catholic life as one long religious high?***

This vision sees Catholic life as a daily experiencing of God and religious experiences as important gifts, giving the person power to live according to the gospel message.

Without such gifts, people won't have the needed help to be a full disciple. They will see the gospel call as unrealistic. They will live out a very weak Christian life.

(E) THE CHURCH'S BELIEF

18) Doesn't the Church already believe in the Conversion Experience?

The Conversion Experience is well explained in many spiritual books which the Church has approved. The Church praises this initial gift and has rules for further spiritual formation.

The Church, in approving these, shows definite belief in this action of God. However, this belief should become more central.

19) What is meant by "becoming more central"?

Right now, the Church's belief in the Conversion Experience is somewhat secondary. These experiences are praised but they are seen as optional. They are for those who happen to want them, or for those who happen to receive them.

The Church does not grasp the importance of the Conversion Experience and does not see this gift as available and vital to every Catholic.

20) Doesn't the Church already preach reform and conversion?

It does but the understanding is very vague and often centers upon moral precepts.

21) What is wrong with centering reform around moral precepts?

The Church should certainly teach clear moral precepts, but that is not the first step to a reform of life.

True conversion follows from an experience of God. Conversion of life follows upon a Conversion Experience. Without faith in this gift of God, Church preaching will present a difficult morality without supplying God's beginning power of conversion.

22) Why does our preaching not center on this Conversion Experience?

In the sixteenth century, Luther and the other Protestant reformers stressed these subjective religious experiences. The Church had to define the importance of objective religious practices, such as, sacraments and liturgical worship.

In the Church, whatever is defined becomes important, and other aspects tend to be overlooked. Since the Council of Trent (which truly saved and revitalized the Church) the stress has been on objective religious practices and the Conversion Experience has been overlooked.

23) Can that be changed?

Now that the Church has clearly taught and defined the central role of the mass and sacraments, the Conversion Experience can once more be safely preached without moving into Protestant heresies.

(F) SCRIPTURAL BASIS

24) *Where does Jesus speak of the Conversion Experience?*

1) His first message is of conversion:
   "This is the time of fulfillment. The reign of God is at hand! Reform your lives and believe in the gospel!" (Mk 1:15)

2) His parables center on the reign of God, on the moment of discovering that Kingdom, and of selling all to obtain it.

   a) The buried treasure.
      "...He hid it again, and rejoicing at his find went and sold all he had and bought that field." (Mt 13:44)

   b) The pearl:
      "When he found one really valuable pearl, he went back and put up for sale all that he had and bought that field." (Mt 13:46)

3) He speaks of the personal changes that will happen from the apostles' new experience:
   "...then your hearts will rejoice
   with a joy no one can take from you."

   (Jn 16:22)

25) *When did the apostles receive their Conversion Experience?*

Their experience was the Easter visions. Through those experiences, they began to see and understand what Jesus had been trying to explain all along.

26) What was their Pentecost Experience?

The Spirit's coming completed their Conversion Experience and prepared them for ministry.

27) Did Peter preach a Conversion Experience?

In concluding his Pentecost sermon, Peter said:

> "...You must reform and be baptized, each one of you, in the name of Jesus Christ, that your sins may be forgiven; then you will receive the gift of the Holy Spirit." (Acts 2:38)

28) Did Paul preach a Conversion Experience?

The following outlines Paul's basic message:

1) He based his ministry upon his own conversion story:

   > "I did not receive it from any man, nor was I schooled in it. It came by revelation from Jesus Christ." (Gal 1:12)

2) He saw the initial converson process as including experiences.

   > "Have you had such remarkable experiences all to no purpose – if indeed they were to no purpose?" (Gal 3:4)

3) These experiences came as a gift.

> "I want to learn only one thing from you; how did you receive the Spirit? Was it through observance of the law or through faith in what you heard?" (Gal 3:2)

4) Salvation is an on-going experience of God's power.

> "The message of the cross is complete absurdity to those who are headed for ruin, but to us who are experiencing salvation it is the power of God." (1 Cor 1:18)

5) Conversion and receiving the Spirit go together:

> "...when you heard the glad tidings of salvation, the word of truth, and believed in it, you were sealed with the Holy Spirit who had been promised." (Eph 1:13)

6) Paul's own life is an on-going experience of Christ:

> "and the life I live now is not my own; Christ is living in me..." (Gal 2:20)

(G) THE MODERN CHURCH

29) *This Conversion Experience might have been necessary in the Early Church. Now, however, people are born into a Catholic culture. Doesn't this Catholic*

culture replace the need for everyone to experience a personal conversion?

It would be a mistake to think the Catholic culture substitutes for the Conversion Experience because:

1) The power of the Catholic culture faces challenges from every side.

2) Sacramental initiation cannot be equated with full Christian initiation. Receiving sacraments of conversion does not automatically bring about a conversion of life.

3) Today, the Conversion Experience needs to be emphasized because of the false assumption that a system (sacramental or educational) can bring about what is really a free gift of God.

30) How does this Conversion Experience differ from a person being converted to the Catholic faith?

A person wishing to join the Church receives Catholic instructions, accepts the truths and is baptized (or formally received). Coupled with that process, there might or might not be a Conversion Experience.

31) What is the relationship of the Conversion Experience with the Rite of Christian Initiation of Adults?

This Rite very much moves into the realm of experiences and stresses the person's own story with God. As such, it can be a clear door into the personal experiences of conversion.

32) *What is needed for the Church to incorporate the Conversion Experience into its daily life?*

The changes must be profound and experienced everywhere in the Church. The Church of teaching and sacraments must also become the Church rooted in God's primary gift of a Conversion Experience. The first changes are within people, both clergy and lay. The other changes, in structure and practice, will come through the Spirit, who never destroys but always restores.

Chapter 4
RELIGIOUS EXPERIENCES

The Apostolic Experience and the Conversion Experience are meant to result in religious experiences, the daily and lifelong experiencing of God's actions.

Like any good relationship, these experiences are fragile. Like communication in marriage, they are difficult to maintain. Like fire, they are indispensable yet always in need of care and protection. Yet, like love itself, they powerfully unite the person to God. When love's fire is extinguished, a coldness sets in and God becomes a far-away figure.

With the discovery of fire, mankind entered a new era. This new era of the Church depends upon the rediscovery of religious experiences, for nothing can take their place.

Religious experiences are God's delight, when He can be Father and Lord and Consoler to His child. They are moments when He reveals Himself, pulling back the veil. They are God's intimacies. Who can measure the glory He receives in revealing Himself to a creature made by His own hand?

If religious experiences are a dangerous terrain, we explore them only because God tells us to, promising that this road will best prepare us for His heavenly revelations.

"Go, reconnoiter the land." (Jos 2:1)

(A) UNDERSTANDING RELIGIOUS EXPERIENCES

1) What are religious experiences?

These experiences are subjective sensations within the person. These sensations extend to all inner faculties (intellect, will, memory and imagination) and to all feelings.

Since true religious experiences are God's activity, the results of these experiences move the person closer to God. They bestow peace, joy, enlightenment and every result associated with God's Spirit.

2) What are Christian religious experiences?

Since Christ is God, all true religious experiences are also Christian. However, since many people who experience God have no personal idea of Jesus Christ, the term, Christian religious experiences, is limited to those experiences where Jesus is consciously acknowledged as Lord.

3) Must God's activity be recognized so an experience can be truly religious?

Not at all. Everyone is moved frequently by God without recognizing His activity.

4) *What value is there in recognizing God as the source?*

There is tremendous value:

1) Jesus condemned the world because it didn't recognize God's work.

> "...the Spirit of truth,
> whom the world cannot accept,
> since it neither sees him nor recognizes him;"
> (Jn 14:17)

2) The special gift to the apostles was their power to see God's inner work:

> "...but you can recognize him
> because he remains with you
> and will be within you." (Jn 14:17)

(B) OPENING THE DOOR

5) *What opens the door to religious experiences?*

This door is called the Conversion Experience, explained in the previous chapter.

6) *What leads a person to this conversion?*

Although God alone bestows the experience, the person's own searching seems to precede the gift.

7) *What makes a person search?*

The regular cause is to hear and respond to preaching. This preaching should open the hearers' hearts to want the Kingdom of God.

"And how can they believe unless they have heard of him? And how can they hear unless there is someone to preach?" (Rom 10:14)

8) Are there other means?

Two basic feelings get people to search for God. The first is a sense of failure, and the second is a sense that life must have more than this world offers.

The sense of failure arises from many causes, such as ill health, economic problems, family disruptions, breakdown in relationships, discouragements, setbacks, etc. The sense that life has more to offer is the beginning of spiritual awakening.

9) What is the next step?

If the person listens to God and seeks a faith solution to his searching, the next step is the Conversion Experience described in the previous chapter.

(C) THE ABIDING GIFT

10) What, then, are religious experiences?

They are the on-going God experiences which follow the Conversion Experience. The Conversion Experience itself is the primary religious experience and the door to a life of religious experiences. (For clarity sake, the beginning experience and the on-going experiences are described separately and given diverse names of Conversion Experience and Religious Experiences.)

11) What if the Conversion Experience is not followed by other religious experiences?

Then God's full purpose in giving the original gift is not fulfilled. In some ways, the person is changed but the daily gift of the Spirit's experiences are lost.

12) Are on-going religious experiences absolutely necessary?

They are absolutely essential for anyone to do great work for God. They also seem important for the ordinary people to fulfill God's task in their own lives.

13) Are religious experiences necessary for salvation?

No claim is made that they are absolutely necessary for personal salvation. Paul distinguishes between a person's work for God and personal salvation.

> "The Day will disclose it. That day will make its appearance with fire and fire will test the quality of each man's work. If the building a man has raised on this foundation still stands, he will receive his recompense; if a man's building burns, he will suffer loss. He himself will be saved, but only as one fleeing through fire." (1 Cor 3:13-15)

14) *If a person has a Conversion Experience but does not cooperate with the religious experience gifts, can he have the Conversion Experience again?*

The Letter to the Hebrews is very pessimistic on this point:

"For when men have once been enlightened and have tasted the heavenly gift and become sharers in the Holy Spirit…and have fallen away, it is impossible to make them repent again.." (6:4-6)

However, the Church has never adopted that pessimism. In practice, the person often cooperates fully at a later time when the conversion gift blossoms into daily religious experiences.

15) *What is the important message in Hebrews?*

Hebrews rightly stresses the importance of the present and of not putting off conversion to a later date. Hebrews says, "Encourage one another daily while it is still 'today'." (3:13)

SCRIPTURAL BASIS

(This chapter shows the importance of religious experiences and stresses the universal availability of this gift through Jesus. The scriptural picture is clear and extensive.)

(D) RELIGIOUS EXPERIENCES IN THE OLD TESTAMENT

(These questions picture the limited role of these experiences in the Old Testament.)

16) How is the Old Testament different from the New Testament?

In the Old Testament, personal religious experiences were deliberately avoided except by God's prophets. Moses explains clearly that people came to God through obedience to a true prophet's word, not by their own experiencing of God.

> "A prophet like me will the Lord, your God, raise up for you from among your own kinsmen; to Him you shall listen. This is exactly what you requested of the Lord, your God, at Horeb on the day of the assembly when you said, 'Let us not again hear the voice of the Lord, our God, nor see this great fire anymore, lest we die.' And the Lord said to me, 'This was well said'." (Dt 18:15-17)

17) Why did the people make that request?

They were frightened by God's manifestations.

> "When the people witnessed the thunder and lightening, the trumpet blast and the mountain smoking, they all feared and trembled. So they took up a position much farther away and said to Moses, 'You speak to us, and we will listen; but let not God speak to us, or we shall die.'" (Ex 20:18-19)

18) Why is this event so important?

It established the basic relationship of the people to God. Moses deliberately recalled the event:

> "The Lord spoke with you face to face on the mountain from the midst of the fire. Since you were afraid of the fire and would not go up the mountain, I stood between the Lord and you at that time, to announce to you these words of the Lord." (Dt 5:4-5)

19) Why are these texts important?

They portray the basic relationship of the Jewish believer to Yahweh. That relationship is marked by fear, distance and the need for the prophet to mediate God's word.

20) Did that relationship ever change?

Although the relationship always remained the same (the prophet giving God's word to the people) the Old Testament contains two doors to the New Testament teaching:

1) The prophets provide a much different idea of God.

2) The prophets speak of an era when all shall enjoy personal religious experiences.

21) *What texts provide a quite different idea of God?*

1) God is seen as Mother:

> "Can a mother forget her infant,
>   be without tenderness for the child of her
>   womb?
> Even should she forget,
>   I will never forget you." (Is 49:15)

2) God is seen as Father:

> "He shall say of me, 'You are my father,
>   my God, the Rock, my saviour'." (Psalm 89:27)

> "He calls blest the destiny of the just
> and boasts that God is his Father."
> (Wis 2:16)

(These texts foresee only the Messiah enjoying a father-son relationship to God.)

22) *What texts prophesy the new era of universal religious experiences?*

Four prophets are important:

1) Ezekiel

> "I will give you a new heart and place
> a new spirit within you.." (36:26)

> "I will put my spirit within you.."
> (36:27)

2) Jeremiah

> "No longer will they have need to teach their friends and kinsmen to know the Lord. All, from the least to the greatest, shall know Me, says the Lord.." (Jer 31:34)

3) Isaiah

> "All your sons shall be taught by the Lord…" (54:13)

4) Joel

> "Your sons and daughters shall prophesy,
>   your old men shall dream dreams,
>   your young men shall see visions;
> Even upon the servants and handmaids,
>   in those days, I will pour out my spirit."
> (3:1-2)

(E) RELIGIOUS EXPERIENCES IN THE NEW TESTAMENT

23) *How does the New Testament differ from the Old?*

The New Testament is different because Jesus enjoys a unique experience of oneness with God. He knows God as His Father and actually shares this gift with the disciples. This gift is for everyone.

24) When does Scripture describe Jesus' unique relationship to the Father?

The following texts teach that relationship:

1) That relationship was from the beginning.

> "In the beginning was the Word;
> The Word was in God's presence,
> and the Word was God." (Jn 1:1)

2) The Father revealed everything to Jesus:

> "For the Father loves the Son
> and everything the Father does he shows him."
> (Jn 5:20)

One text shows the Jews understood Jesus' unique claims. They were determined to kill him because He "was speaking of God as his own Father, thereby making himself God's equal." (Jn 5:18)

25) What texts show Jesus' power to share His religious experiences?

Jesus makes the following claims:

1) He is the only source of true religious experiences:

> "I am the way, and the truth, and the life;
> no one comes to the Father but through me."
> (Jn 14:5)

2) He alone can bestow knowledge of the Father:

> "No one knows the Son but the Father, and no one knows the Father but the Son – and anyone to whom the Son wishes to reveal Him." (Mt 11:27)

3) Experiencing Him is the same as experiencing the Father:

> "Whoever has seen me has seen the Father." (Jn 14:9)

4) The experience is the same because He abides in the Father.

> "How can you say, 'Show us the Father'? Do you not believe that I am in the Father and the Father is in me?" (Jn 14:9-10)

26) *What is the New Testament picture of believers sharing in religious experiences?*

1) Jesus promises a full revealing.

> "I too will love Him and reveal myself to Him." (Jn 14:21)

2) All will participate in Jesus' gift.

> "Of His fullness we have all had a share – love following upon love." (Jn 1:16)

3) Jesus fulfills the Isaiah prophecy (54:13) concerning religious experiences.

> "It is written in the prophets:
> 'They shall all be taught by God.'
> Everyone who has heard the Father
> and learned from Him
> comes to me." (Jn 6:45)

4) The Pentecost outpouring is seen by Peter as fulfilling Joel's prophecy of religious experiences.

> "No, it is what Joel the prophet spoke
> of:" (Acts 2:16)

27) How did Jesus make religious experiences available to all believers?

Jesus sent the Spirit who first made us God's children and then bestowed experiences of sonship.

1) The Spirit made us God's children.

> "See what love the Father has bestowed on us
> in letting us be called children of God!
> Yet that is what we are." (1 Jn 3:1)

2) He then bestowed experiences of sonship.

> "The proof that you are sons is the
> fact that God has sent forth into our
> hearts the spirit of His Son which cries
> out 'Abba!' ('Father!')." (Gal 4:6)

(F)   ROLE OF JESUS

28)   Don't people experience God apart from Jesus Christ?

Since the Father so much wants all people to experience Him, everyone can enjoy religious experiences. To make these experiences available to all, the Father gave us Jesus.

29)   What advantage is there in believing in Jesus?

1)   Jesus bestows these experiences on all believers.

2)   With Jesus, the person is safe with these experiences.

3)   With Jesus the person will have the guidance of the Church.

30)   Isn't the claim that all believers in Jesus should enjoy religious experiences an exaggerated one?

When compared to the Old Testament, the New Testament claim is unique. Yet the picture is clear. Jesus shares with every believer His own relationship and experience of the Father. This gift is "hidden from the learned and the clever" and "revealed to the merest children." (Mt 11:25)

31)   Why must there be sure guidance in religious experiences?

No world is more dangerous than the path of religious experiences. Human history shows the havoc wreaked by invalid religious experiences (wars, mass suicides, personal problems).

32) How does Jesus provide these needed safeguards?

A believer doesn't enter this path alone. He is accompanied by the balanced picture of Jesus Himself in the gospels, by the instructions contained in the New Testament letters, by the Church, and by the religious traditions of other holy people who have enjoyed these religious gifts.

33) Moses said that he stood between the Lord and the people. How is this any different from the role of Jesus?

The New Testament teaches that experiencing Jesus is the same as experiencing the Father. The same can't be said of Moses. Hebrews states that Moses was faithful to God "but Jesus is more worthy of honor than he, as the founder of a house is more honorable than the house itself." (3:3)

The initial Old Testament relationship (symbolized by Moses) has been completely surpassed in Jesus. Moses stood between God and the people. Jesus is God. Seeing Him is seeing the Father.

34) Does Paul speak about this contrast?

Very clearly. He speaks about Moses' face being veiled and "only in Christ that it (veil) is taken away." (2 Cor 3:12-14). He concludes with a statement about religious experiences. "All of us, gazing on the Lord's glory with unveiled faces, are being transformed from glory to glory into his very image by the Lord who is the Spirit." (3:18)

35) What is the Church's role?

The Church is the usual place to receive and grow in religious experiences. Therefore, a person who receives private religious experiences should seek out Church guidance.

If religious experiences pull a person away from the Church, then these experiences are being falsely interpreted. Religious experiences should be regularly submitted to the discernment of Church leaders and correction willingly accepted.

(G) HISTORY OF RELIGIOUS EXPERIENCES

36) What is the history of religious experiences in the Catholic Church?

That history is somewhat similar to the history of the charisms. The Early Church abounded in the religious experiences of the Easter visions and the Pentecostal outpouring.

As time wore on, religious experiences faded into the background and the more institutional forms of Catholicism emerged. However, there has always been a strong, hidden stream of religious experiences.

37) What were the manifestations of this stream?

The religious experience stream constantly burst forth in movements. Some of these movements went astray. Others stayed within Catholic teaching and enriched the Church.

38) What were some of these movements?

1) The hermit movement with St. Anthony as the founder (3rd and 4th centuries).

2) The monastic movements begun by St. Basil (4th century) and by St. Benedict (5th century).

3) The Mendicant Orders of St. Francis of Assisi and St. Dominic (13th century).

4) The active religious of St. Ignatius and St. Vincent de Paul (16th and 17th centuries).

Besides the above, there were pietist movements which enriched the Church with the rosary, the stations of the cross, devotions to the Sacred Heart, and now, frequent communion.

(H) TODAY'S CHURCH

39) Doesn't the Church have the means of fostering religious experiences?

The Church has many means, such as retreats, days of recollection, devotions, and especially the liturgy itself.

40) Why aren't these sufficient?

If every Catholic were experiencing a deep personal life of prayer, then these means would certainly be adequate. However, that is not the case. A large percentage of Catholics don't even attend Mass.

41) Couldn't it be concluded that those who do attend Mass are experiencing God?

That conclusion would be gratuitous. Unfortunately, some Catholics leave the Church precisely because they find their religious experiences in a Protestant church or bible study group. Some Catholics, through Church movements or through personal endeavor, do enter into the religious experience gift. However, many Catholics remain untouched.

42) Why is this so?

Fostering religious experiences is not a primary goal of the Catholic Church. As a result, every effort is not made to bring about and foster these experiences.

43) Why not?

Their importance has not been grasped.

44) What are the goals in the Catholic Church?

The ultimate goals are salvation and sanctification. The primary goals are Catholic education and the reception of the sacraments, usually at the parish level. Secondary goals include social services, ecumenism, and social justice.

45) If religious experiences were a primary goal, what would change at the parish level?

First, those involved in pastoral care would themselves have to be experiencing God. Without this, every effort to foster religious experiences is doomed to failure.

Secondly, the people must be told that they can and should experience God.

Thirdly, time, effort, and money would be devoted to fostering religious experiences.

46) *Why do those leading a parish need to experience God?*

Without those experiences, they can do little to help others. They would have little idea of what to do or what is involved. Without experiencing the gift, they would have little enthusiasm for, or even perseverence in fostering religious experiences.

47) *Why must they believe that the people can and should experience God?*

People act from their beliefs. If pastoral leaders believe that the people can experience God, they will make efforts. If they grasp the importance of these experiences, they will make a lot of effort. The results will follow.

48) *Just what efforts would be made?*

The primary effort must focus on the Sunday liturgy. However, there would also have to be other efforts during the week to teach, encourage, and nourish these experiences.

(I) RELIGIOUS EXPERIENCES AND CATHOLIC PENTECOSTAL RENEWAL

49) Would people have to pray in tongues?

Widescale, sustained religious experiences are impossible without praying in tongues. The lack of religious experiences is due to the absence of praying in tongues.

50) Would everyone have to be baptized in the Spirit?

It would be the other way around. As religious experiences are fostered and received, people would realize they had received the Baptism in the Spirit. The term itself may or may not be used to express the beginning religious experience gift.

51) Will such widescale religious experiences ever occur?

Decades ago, before the distractions of the modern world, when life was at a slower pace, many Catholics experienced God in their private devotions. Now, people's thoughts are constantly bombarded by the mass media. God experiences have been replaced by radio, television, alcohol and drug experiences.

With the present teachings and practices, widescale religious experiences will not occur. The Church can never create again the slower pace of life that existed decades ago. However, if the Church rediscovers religious experiences, then widescale experiences can happen even in the modern world.

52) *What are the options?*

There are two basic options:

The Church can allow the modern world to claim an ever greater share of peoples' experiences and allow secularization to have complete power. Or, the Church can refuse to be passive in the face of powerful worldly experiences and can decide to release the rich reserves of religious experiences placed within each believer through the Sacrament of Baptism.

Chapter 5
THE IMPORTANCE OF A SCRIPTURAL MENTALITY

The Church's primary goal is to sanctify God's people. "You, however, are a chosen race, a royal priesthood, a holy nation…" (1 Pt 2:9). An often forgotten and set aside power to sanctify is the reading of Scripture.

The tremendous committal of Catholic monks to keep alive the bible by copying manuscripts was not followed through by the later Church. The discovery of the printing press preceded Luther, allowing him to capitalize on the bible's widespread availability. As a result, the Scriptures were stolen from our hands.

Carrying and reading the bible is now clearly associated with Protestantism. Catholics rightly say that they have sacraments, liturgy, prayer books and catechisms. Yet something very important is missing when Catholics are not put directly in touch with God's Holy Word. A formation of personality and mentality are direct effects of a taste for Scripture.

The bible shows God acting and people responding (correctly or incorrectly). The New Testament has letters rooted in a belief in Jesus and His Spirit. The Old Testament has wisdom sayings, psalms and proverbs. The entire bible collects various streams of religious experiences whose source is the revealing God.

Every author writes to form and influence his readers. God, however, both acted and recorded His own activity so all mankind could be formed into His people. The bible is a special book containing God's power. No other book can bestow a scriptural mentality.

Enjoying a scriptural mentality means people have entered through a special door. They have begun to see their life, their decisions, and their experiences from God's perspective. Without this scriptural mentality religious experiences are lost and never completed. The God of these experiences is also the author of the bible. After bestowing the experiences, He expects us to be formed by His book.

Personal scriptural reading and religious experiences go together. Experiences bestow a desire to read God's Word. The reading in turn fosters, keeps alive, and completes the experiences.

(A) UNDERSTANDING THE SCRIPTURAL MENTALITY

1) What is a scriptural mentality?

A scriptural mentality is a habit of mind and pattern of thought formed by regular contact with God's actions in Scripture.

2) What is a habit of mind?

It is the subconscious way the person approaches the questions and decisions of each day. The subconscious draws upon all the stored memories and developed mental habits.

3) What is a thought pattern?

That pattern is a person's complete way of thinking. It includes language, vocabulary, ideas, goals, motives and everything else that forms a person's thought processes.

A scriptural mentality would presuppose that the vocabulary, ideas and goals of the bible are already part of the person's thinking.

4) Where do people receive their pattern of thought?

This pattern comes from every external influence and from every internal decision. Patterns begin forming at birth and continue throughout life. Primary influences are the family, the school, the church and the culture.

(B) IMPORTANCE OF THIS GIFT

5) What is the present state of our culture?

Our present culture is extremely powerful, and unfortunately not rooted in family or neighborhood values. Through the mass media and a constantly shifting population, children have experiences far beyond the family. Insuring that the child's culture is filled with only the finest elements is now impossible.

6) Why is a scriptural mentality important?

This mentality, formed according to God's Spirit, is a powerful force in discerning and purifying the pervasive influences of the world's culture.

7) Doesn't a scriptural mentality mean Fundamentalism and bible-banging

The bible-banging mentality is just the opposite of a true scriptural mentality. Bible-banging means that denominational truths are defended and preached. Scriptural texts are used as proofs for these truths. This approach does not enter into the true picture of scripture, but approaches the bible with a pre-formed mentality.

(C)   ELEMENTS OF THIS MENTALITY

8) What are the intellectual elements of a scriptural mentality?

A scriptural mentality means that the believer:

1) has absorbed the basic scriptural doctrines.

2) is acquainted with the various wisdom sayings, teachings and scriptural stories.

9) What are the basic teachings?

These teachings include the following truths:

1) God exists. He is an all-powerful force helping the person to life's goal.

2) He is a personal Father, Who intervenes, helps and expects a response to His fatherhood.

3) God has intervened in His Son, Jesus.

4) Jesus has sent the Holy Spirit Who unites the believer to the Father. The Spirit is each person's teacher and consoler.

5) The Spirit formed the Church, which is God's gift to help the person.

6) Each person is called to a new life in the Spirit.

7) Fidelity to this life culminates in eternal happiness.

10) Why are the wisdom sayings, teachings and stories important?

These sayings, teachings and stories provide concrete, powerful images. Conscious behavior is formed and shaped by our subconscious images. These images, lying deep within, often hidden and forgotten, have a daily effect on choices.

11) How do they exercise this effect?

A person is free only within limits. For example, an individual cannot suddenly speak a foreign language, but must slowly fill his mind with the new vocabulary words and new patterns of thought. A transformation into a Christian life demands that the subconscious be daily filled with scriptural images.

(D) BEGINNING THE MENTALITY

12) *How do people acquire a scriptural mentality?*

They must read the Bible which contains the stories, categories of thought, values and goals inspired by God Himself. These elements must enter into both the person's mentality and the thought pattern of their Catholic parish.

13) *Why must both the person and the parish be formed by scripture?*

The scriptural mentality should form both the believer and the believing Church. Through this mentality, the believer internalizes the bible's goals and God's thought. By many people enjoying this mentality, a whole culture is brought forth that supports the individual. Ideally, this scripturally formed community is the local parish.

(E) SCRIPTURAL BASIS

14) *What parts of this teaching are clearly taught in scripture?*

Scripture clearly teaches the following:

1) The believer should experience a new understanding.

2) This new mentality is needed to overcome the world's thinking.

3) This new understanding comes only through God's inner action.

4) The new understanding should form the believing community.

15) What texts highlight need for a new understanding?

Jesus expected a new understanding:

1) "Are you, too, incapable of understanding?" (Mk 7:18)

2) "He summoned the crowd and said to them: 'Give ear and try to understand.' " (Mt 15:10)

Paul expected a changed attitude:

1) "Your attitude must be that of Christ." (Phil 2:5)

2) "But we have the mind of Christ." (1 Cor 2:16)

16) What texts stress an overcoming of the world's thinking?

The following clearly show this goal:

1) "Do not conform yourselves to this age but be transformed by the renewal of your mind..." (Rom 12:2)

2) "I am talking about those who are set upon the things of this world. As you well know, we have our citizenship in heaven..." (Phil 3:19)

17) What texts stress that this new understanding comes only from God's inner action?

Paul speaks clearly of Christ's role in this new understanding:

> "To this day, when the old covenant is read the veil remains unlifted; it is only in Christ that it is taken away." (2 Cor 3:14)

God's wisdom is too deep for mere human understanding:

> "How deep are the riches and the wisdom and the knowledge of God. How inscrutable his judgments and how unsearchable his ways." (Rom 11:33)

18) ***What texts show that reading God's word should also form the believing community?***

1) In the New Testament, the call to be God's people began with a preaching of God's word:

> "The word of God continued to spread..." (Acts 6:7)

> "All through Judea the apostles and the brothers heard that the Gentiles, too, had accepted the word of God." (Acts 11:1)

> "Thus did the word of the Lord continue to spread with influence and power." (Acts 19:20)

2) After the original call, God's word continues its power:

> "Your rebirth has come, not from a destructible but from an indestructible seed, through the living and enduring word of God." (1 Pet 1:23)

3) The final result is God's people:

> "Once you were no people, but now you are God's people." (1 Pet 2:10)

19) What texts show that Jesus' own mentality was filled with the Scriptures?

These texts are abundant. They show Jesus' own mentality was rooted in the Old Testament. Jesus uses Scripture

1) to overcome Satan on three occasions. (Mt 4:1-11)

2) to describe John the Baptist. (Mt 11:10)

3) to justify His actions against the money changers. (Mt 21:12)

4) to prophesy Peter's denial. (Mt 26:31)

5) to prophesy His own passion. (Mk 9:12)

6) to proclaim Himself as anointed with the Spirit. (Lk 4:21)

Jesus going with the two disciples to Emmaus showed his scriptural mentality

> "Beginning then, with Moses and all the prophets, he interpreted for them every passage of Scripture which referred to him." (Lk 24:27)

Jesus also spoke of the perduring power of scripture:

> "...and Scripture cannot lose its force..." (Jn 10:35)

(F) ROLE OF RELIGIOUS EXPERIENCES

20) How does a person acquire a taste for scripture reading?

A desire to read scripture is a fruit of religious experiences. Without the beginning conversion experiences, the person, no matter how educated, will always be unable to enter fully into the scriptural treasures.

21) Why are religious experiences and scripture reading so closely connected?

Both are the work of the same Holy Spirit. Sometimes the Spirit moves a person to read scripture, and through that reading, bestows religious experiences. At other times, the Spirit first touches the person with experiences. Through these experiences, the person thirsts to read scripture. Both religious experiences and reading scripture are needed for true growth. Experiences without scripture or reading scripture without experiences is not enough.

22) Do Catholics in the Renewal have both religious experiences and scripture reading?

Newcomers are brought quickly into religious experiences. Through these experiences they begin to read the scripture more regularly. Also, spontaneous bible readings are a regular part of the prayer meetings.

Unfortunately, this bible reading does not occur as much as among Protestant Pentecostals.

23) Why not as often as among the Protestant Pentecostals?

First, bible reading is more accentuated in Protestant Churches. The Catholic charismatic comes from a Church which only recently has stressed the importance of bible reading. This emphasis is still weak.

Second, even within this Catholic Renewal, personal bible reading is not stressed enough.

24) Doesn't the Catholic Church stress the scripture readings in the daily liturgy?

A liturgical bible reading is quite different from a personal reading. At liturgy, the person is passive. The reading is part of the worship. Liturgical reading has little impact in moving the person to pick up the bible on his/her own.

25) Why is this personal reading important?

The bible, like any book, is a constant invitation. In the very hectic modern world, the bible provides a shelter and refuge. It is a place of refreshment and calm. Reading the scriptures turns the person from secular experiences to stories of God experiences.

26) How does bible reading lead to a scriptural mentality?

A person's language, mental images, values and goals are influenced by the environment. Scripture introduces God's stories and God's thinking into that environment.

By reading scripture, the person deliberately chooses to have God's word instead of television ads, newspapers, magazines and all the world's influences.

(G) OBJECTIONS

(Discussing objections to the scriptural mentality will also highlight its positive factors.)

27) *Should not Catholics center on a study of the Apostles Creed and the traditional teachings of the Church?*

The Church has developed its creed and teachings from scripture. However, the Church doesn't intend that Catholics set aside the scriptural books and stories in which the Creed is rooted.

28) *Would not Catholics, if they got deeply involved in scriptures, gradually give Church truths a secondary place?*

A scriptural mentality is quite different from a scripture alone attitude. The Catholic reading scripture isn't asked to give up Church truths, or to adopt only the scriptural stories. The two are meant to go together.

29) *Isn't it a danger that Catholics would fall into a scripture alone mentality?*

If the scripture reading is done in a Protestant culture (bible study group or non-denominational teaching), the danger is very real. This is because a Protestant group is usually rooted in a scripture only mentality. That danger is not present if the fostering of scriptural reading takes place in a Catholic atmosphere.

30) Does the average person have enough time to read Scripture?

Doesn't the average person read the newspaper, watch television, page through magazines and even read novels or other books on a daily or regular basis? Obviously, the problem has nothing to do with the amount of time available for reading.

31) Would not the person get lost in Scripture, or wander doctrinally, confused by what they might find?

If a person is doctrinally troubled or trying to solve faith problems by finding scriptural answers, they should stay away from the scriptures. Instead, they should present their problems to a priest.

The average Catholic would not be confused but would find much help for their life in the bible.

(G) NEEDED ELEMENTS

32) What is needed to gain a Scriptural Mentality?

The person must:

1) enter the door of religious experiences.

2) be trying to live as a Christian.

3) receive some help in this reading.

4) be involved with others who are also trying to live by the scriptures.

33) Why are religious experiences necessary?

Until the person experiences God's inner actions there is little attraction to read the scriptures. Without these experiences, the person sees the bible as a literary work or the dull, albeit inspired, word of God. Scripture is literally a closed book which probably has a place of honor in the home but not in the heart.

After religious experiences, the person has a new taste for scriptural reading, sometimes even an unquenchable desire.

These religious experiences are needed to sustain this desire. The bible, although very readable, has no natural attraction which can make someone a daily reader for life. The regular attraction to read comes from daily religious experiences.

34) Why must the person be trying to live as a Christian?

The bible is direction for the journey, and a constant help in coming to God. A person who isn't trying to walk with God, has no real interest in the main purpose of scriptural reading, and no real motives to read the bible daily. Most people don't bother to read a map unless they are going to travel.

35) Why does the person need help and encouragement?

The modern world makes too many demands upon people's time. Without outside encouragement, these demands will not be overcome and the daily reading of scripture will be gradually, but totally set aside.

36) When should the Catholic receive this help and encouragement?

This help should come at the Sunday liturgy. Anything else will touch only a small percentage of parishioners.

Catholics should either bring their bibles to Church (an astounding thought) or have bibles provided by the parish. By following the liturgy, they would become used to reading from the bible.

37) Does this not go against some liturgists who want God's Word proclaimed?

A goal of liturgical renewal is clear proclamation. A deeper goal is that Catholics read God's Word. Currently, this deeper goal is not really happening. The average Catholic is not stirred to read scripture during the week by having scripture read on Sunday. Some scriptural renewal is taking place in small meetings on other evenings. However, whatever isn't fostered at the Sunday liturgy, will never touch any significant percentage of Catholics.

38) Why does the person need others who are also living by a Scriptural Mentality?

Everyone is deeply affected by their relationships. Gathering with others in bible reading would stir people to a private reading. The Church is supposed to be the People of God living under His Word. The more active God's Word is, the more the Church will truly be His people.

Chapter 6
NEED FOR A THEOLOGY OF THE SPIRIT

A Catholic theology is a system of thought trying to explain God's actions which began at creation, continued in the Old Testament, and culminated in the Final Age when Jesus sent His Spirit. Just as God revealed Himself in human history, so theology develops in the Church's history. These thought systems are human understandings of God's actions adapted to the questions of the day.

The first theology was worked out by St. Paul. It was his attempt to enlighten all men on the mysterious design hidden for all ages in God, the Creator of all. (Eph 33:9) Later, such writers as St. Justin (2nd century), St. Augustine (4th century) and St. Thomas Aquinas (13th century) tried to explain Christian truths to the people of their day.

In the 16th century, the Council of Trent used St. Thomas' writings. At the beginning of the 20th century, Pope Leo XIII brought about a revival of St. Thomas as the foundation of all seminary training. Therefore, Catholic theology depends on and receives its intellectual strength from St.

Thomas. In the last few decades, new systems of theology have sought more modern sources for explaining Catholic truths.

This chapter is not a theological criticism of St. Thomas, nor of recent theological speculation. It is a strong plea for a development of a theology of the Holy Spirit. Thomas, when teaching about the Spirit, centers mostly on the Spirit's role within the Trinity, while speaking little of His role in salvation. Most modern scholars have not seen a theology of Spirit as central.

If Jesus' Sending of the Spirit, the Apostolic Experience, and the Conversion Experience are not to be lost to Catholics, then the Church needs a theology of the Spirit.

A) UNDERSTANDING A THEOLOGY

1) What is a Catholic theology?

A Catholic theology is the way an author tries to explain the various truths and practices of the Church.

2) Why is such an explanation important?

If the explanation is clear and modern, then people will more easily accept the truths. If the explanation is poor, or out of touch, then that theology will present obstacles to belief.

3) Is the Church always changing its theology?

Since theology is an explanation of truths, the Church allows theologians the freedom to explain Catholic belief in the best possible way. In this sense, theology is always developing.

4) Why should there be constant theological development?

Mankind is constantly changing. The Church's theology must keep in contact with these changes so that the Church is not proclaiming its message in a way people can't understand.

B) THOMISTIC THEOLOGY

5) Does not the Church have a "perennial theology", a system that has been used for centuries?

The Church's perennial theology is based upon Thomas Aquinas' explanation in the 13th century. His theology was used extensively by the Council of Trent in the 16th century and provided the basis for the Baltimore Catechism.

6) What is wrong with Thomistic Theology?

Nothing is wrong with that theology. It is a brilliant synthesis of the Church's thinking up until the 13th century. That its teachings are still the most important theological basis for the modern Church evidences its power and clarity.

7) Why the need, then, for a theology of the Spirit?

Thomas' theology centered on Jesus Christ, the Word made Flesh, and the sacramental system. His writings contain little about the Spirit, especially regarding the Spirit's actions in our midst.

His Book Three (Summa Theologica) has fifty-nine chapters about Jesus Christ, but none of them deals with Jesus sending the Spirit.

C) MODERN THEOLOGIANS

8) *What do modern theologians center on?*

Even today, the overwhelming number of theology texts deal with Christ and a small handful with the Holy Spirit. There have been pleas for a theology of the Spirit, but the primary focus in the Western Church remains focused on Christ.

9) *What is wrong with a central focus on Jesus Christ?*

If this focus results in a weak theology of the Spirit which places the Spirit's activity in a very secondary, almost optional role, then the Church will suffer drastically from a loss of power.

10) *Why is a theology so important?*

If a theology is not developed, the power of this Pentecostal Renewal will be lost. It is as simple as that.

The Catholic Church is not guided by experiences or by events but by its theology. The hierarchical Church tests experiences, even widespread and popular ones. It is the Rock of Peter and is not "carried about by every wind of doctrine." (Eph 4:14)

However, if these religious experiences are accompanied by a clear theology, then the Church will accept and integrate that teaching into its own message.

D) EFFECTS OF THEOLOGY

11) What effect would this theology have?

Within the Church, theology sets the tone. Because of theology's power and importance, the Church carefully watches the theologians. A theology enunciates truths which confront the whole Church. The Holy Spirit will never renew the Church until a theology of the Spirit confronts the present theologies and modifies them.

12) Why is this so?

Our current theologies tend to stop with Jesus. However, the Father's gift to mankind was only completed by Jesus sending His Spirit. Any theology that includes only the Father sending Jesus, is dealing with only two members of the Trinity. Many important elements are missing.

13) What is the basic message of theologies centered on Christ?

These theologies say that Jesus founded the Church and instituted the sacraments. He is also seen as ratifying the Ten Commandments and preaching the Beatitudes.

These give the impression that Catholic life means belonging to the Church, receiving the sacraments and keeping the commandments. The Beatitudes are seen as the New Law of Christ.

14) What is missing?

Missing entirely from this schema are the Spirit's actions. The Spirit's activity is acknowledged but no theology takes

His actions seriously. No theology sees the Spirit's sending as ushering in a new era.

In plain words, when Christ is the center, then the actions of Christ are seen as central. The actions of the Spirit are viewed as secondary, optional and minimally important.

15) Why does this happen?

A theology of Christ which does not include His sending the Spirit highlights what has already happened. Theology is seen as explaining historical events and the historical teachings of the Church.

Only a theology which includes the Spirit's sending can speak fully about the present. The Spirit is the power of God acting in our midst.

E) NEED FOR THEOLOGY OF SPIRIT

16) Why is this theology needed now?

In the modern world, power alone has meaning. Powerless truths mean nothing. A theology which is only academic, even if it carefully and cleverly explains Catholic truths, is meaningless.

Only a theology which opens the door of God's power has meaning to the world today. An appeal for a theology of the Spirit is not a request for an intellectual approach to the Third Person of the Trinity. It is a plea for a theology that releases God's power in the Church.

17) How can a theology release God's power?

A clear theology molds God's revelations and the Church's experiences into a clear message. A theology should bestow light, explaining what is important and what the Church should be doing. That is the theologian's gift.

A clear theology of the Spirit would result in the Church understanding and seeking God's power.

18) Doesn't the Church even now seek God's power?

The Church certainly seeks God's power according to its present understanding. A theology should focus that understanding. If theology is confusing, then the Church loses God's power. If a theology is true, then the Church knows better how to find God's power for the people.

F) SCRIPTURAL BASIS

(The following questions are meant to show that St. Paul based his theology on the belief that the new age of the Spirit was God's power in our midst.)

19) What was Paul's theology?

All the key texts in Paul show his theology was rooted in God's power.

    1)   The theme in Romans shows his belief.

        "I am not ashamed of the gospel. It is the power of God leading everyone who believes in it to salvation, the Jew first, then the Greek." (Rom 1:16)

2) Power is the foundation of his ministry.

   "My message and my preaching had none of the persuasive force of 'wise' argumentation, but the convincing power of the Spirit. As a consequence, your faith rests not on the wisdom of men but on the power of God." (1 Cor 2:4 & 5)

3) He trusts God's power, not his own.

   "And so I willingly boast of my weaknesses instead, that the power of Christ may rest upon me." (2 Cor 12:9)

4) He sees the powerlessness of other theologies.

   "Now that you have come to know God—or rather, have been known by him—how can you return to those powerless, worthless, natural elements to which you seem willing to enslave yourselves once more?" (Gal 4:9)

5) He condemns those who preach a different source of God's power:

   "I repeat what I have just said: if anyone preaches a gospel to you other than the one you received, let a curse be upon him!" (Gal 1:9)

20) Where does Paul speak of God's power within the person?

The following texts show Paul's faith in God's inner actions.

1) Within each believer:

"May He enlighten your innermost vision that you may know...the immeasurable scope of his power in us who believe." (Eph 1:18-19)

2) Within Paul himself:

"I wish to know Christ and the power flowing from his resurrection..." (Phil 3:10)

3) God's power freeing Paul:

"What a wretched man I am! Who can free me from this body under the power of death? All praise to God, through Jesus Christ our Lord!" (Rom 7:24-25)

21) Why should theology highlight God's power?

The whole New Testament announces one truth. God's power has entered human history in Jesus Christ who sent His Spirit. Every theology should explain that single truth. People must be invited to seek that power and live under God's power. Theology's many parts are all just streams flowing from the same river, the power of God in Jesus.

22) Doesn't Paul write of many things besides God's power?

Yes, but everywhere he writes in the light of the truth of God's power in our midst. For example:

1) He criticizes the law because it is powerless. (Rom Ch. 8)

2) He demands high moral standards because God's power is now available. (Eph Ch. 5; Col Ch. 3)

3) He sees clearly the beginning of a new age as God's power is revealed. (Eph Ch. 3)

4) He interprets all history in light of God's power in Jesus Christ. (Letter to the Romans)

23) Where did Paul receive this theology?

His theology flowed from his experience of Jesus. Paul wrote:

"I did not receive it from any man, nor was I schooled in it. It came by revelation from Jesus Christ." (Gal 1:12)

He constantly recounted his own conversion story on the way to Damascus as the foundation of his preaching.

24) Did Paul get into any battles because of his theology?

The New Testament recounts Paul's continuous battle against great odds. If Paul had lost this theological battle, then the power of Jesus' sending the Spirit would have been stifled.

"I will not treat God's gracious gift as pointless. If justice is available through the law, then Christ died to no purpose!" (Gal 2:21)

G) ROLE OF PENTECOSTAL THEOLOGY

25) *Isn't a theology of the Spirit merely a theology of Pentecostal Renewal?*

The two are quite different. A Pentecostal theology explains religious experiences, charismatic powers and gifts. A theology of the Spirit explains all revelation.

A Pentecostal theology has a narrow focus. A theology of the Spirit involves every part of God's revelation and the Church's teachings.

26) *Isn't that too wide a claim for any theology of the Spirit?*

A theology that would merely explain the Spirit's role in the Trinity and His Pentecostal manifestations would forget that the Spirit shares with the Father and the Son in every external work of the Trinity.

27) *What is the role of Pentecostal Renewal in forming a theology of the Spirit?*

This Renewal highlights the subjective, personal aspects in the Spirit-believer relationship. This part is often missing. This Renewal stresses that sacraments exist to bestow the Spirit; that commandments are impossible burdens without the Spirit's help, that the Church exists for one reason— to foster the Spirit within every person. The Spirit is everywhere. A theology that doesn't see this pervading Guest can't be a life-giving word.

Theology should be the stream described in Revelation.

> "The angel then showed me the river of life-giving water, clear as crystal, which issued from the throne of God and of the Lamb and flowed down the middle of the streets." (Rev 22:1)

In the Catholic Church, "the middle of the streets" means the theology that she embraces and preaches.

Section Two
The Renewal Itself

Chapter 7
UNIVERSALITY
OF THE PENTECOSTAL
RENEWAL

Only a handful of Catholics were personally involved in the Liturgical Renewal. The same is true of the Ecumenical Movement. Yet all Catholics have now been affected by both. By entering into mainstream Catholicism, the gifts of these Renewals have become universal.

This chapter focuses on the questions of universality. How extensive does God intend this Renewal to become? Who can correctly read the "signs of the times"? What should be examined to see if this Renewal is for everyone? In talking about universality, certainly numerical growth or decline has to be considered and the experiences of these almost two decades taken into account.

At present, the universality of this Renewal seems a far-off dream. It was different in the early years (1967 to 1975). Then the growth was "wildfire", with ever increasing numbers at charismatic conferences, and ever expanding prayer groups and prayer communities. Since then, the bulging numbers have not happened.

No matter what the numerical picture, universality is a tantalizing thought. It opens dreams of what might be and spurs everyone on to bold plans and trust. Did not the Early Church, in its very smallness and weaknesses, dare to dream of itself as a gift to the whole world?

(A) REASONS AGAINST UNIVERSALITY

1) What does "universality" mean?

The word means for everyone. A universal renewal means that everyone is affected by the powers of this Renewal.

2) Does that mean everyone should join a prayer group?

The prayer group structure is really too fragile to include everyone. Universality cannot come about by every Catholic joining a prayer group.

3) Why is the prayer group structure too fragile?

The prayer groups lack too many needed qualities to be able to contain and care for every Catholic. A quick look at prayer groups show:

1) They meet on a weekday evening.

2) Their leaders often can guide only a small group.

3) They frequently suffer from lack of leadership.

4) They lack the pastoral discernment for the powerful gifts.

4) Why does the weekday evening militate against universality?

In the pace of modern life (especially in the United States), the churches have managed, at least to date, to have Sunday mornings set aside as the weekly time for religious practice.

Whatever religious worship takes place at any other time will never attract even a significant percentage of believers.

5) Why can leaders only guide a small group?

In charismatic prayer, leading 10 is quite different than leading 30. With each noticeable increase (30 to 75 to 150) there are required greater charismatic and personal gifts.

Many times prayer groups have grown large but have not maintained that growth because the leaders did not have the spiritual and pastoral gifts necessary to lead these larger numbers.

6) Why do groups suffer from lack of leadership?

Charismatic leadership is so new that it is often not clear just who is a good leader and who is not. Expectations can often be unrealistic. Also, groups are isolated and lack the help needed from a diocesan organization.

As now structured, prayer groups so much rise and fall upon the personal qualities and relationships of leaderships, that they cannot embrace every Catholic.

7) Why are powerful gifts and discernment needed?

Currently, the attractions to the weekly prayer group are the charisms. Powerful charisms lead to larger attendance.

However, the more powerful the charisms, the greater need for discernment and for quality pastoral care.

In most groups, leaders would not know how to handle either the powerful charisms nor the crowds these charisms attract.

8) Should the prayer group structure be strengthened?

Certainly the prayer group structure should be strengthened in every way possible. However, no amount of strengthening will ever bring the prayer groups to a point where they are the foundation for a universal outpouring of the Spirit.

9) Would the answer be regional prayer groups where the needed gifts and leadership qualities could be present?

Regional gatherings can strengthen the prayer group structure. However, the more the Renewal moves away from the local scene, the less it can bring about universality.

10) From the current evidence, it appears that this Renewal is not universal.

Certainly, the current state of the Renewal cannot become a universal phenomenon. Although some people have been deeply touched and committed to the Renewal for years, these represent a very small percentage of the Church. Many others have never been involved and some Catholics would not even want to be involved.

(B) REASONS FOR UNIVERSALITY

11) *What points to the universality of this Renewal?*

Any claim for universality is based upon an understanding of the Renewal's theology, teaching and experience. As these are grasped they should be seen as for everyone and not limited to a particular group.

12) *How is the Renewal's theology a basis for universality?*

This Renewal's doctrinal basis is Jesus' Sending the Spirit. All the other doctrines associated with Pentecostal theology are rooted in this primary truth.

13) *How does that theology argue for a universality?*

Since Sending the Spirit marks the Final Age of God's actions in history, that truth is extremely important for everyone. The Renewal is proclaiming, acting upon, and experiencing the central truth of the Final Age.

(C) REASONS FOR UNIVERSALITY FROM THE TEACHING

14) *Doesn't the Church, in her theology and doctrine, also proclaim the same truth?*

This primacy of the Spirit is often overlooked, taken for granted, or pushed into the background. The Renewal is like the merchant who has come upon the pearl of a great price.

15) How can this pearl be described?

The following would be a core description of Pentecostal understanding:

1) The Church can be renewed through religious experiences.

2) These experiences are abundant when they are sought.

3) Seeking these experiences comes from a living faith in the Spirit being sent by Jesus.

4) When religious experiences are manifested, the Spirit extends his primacy over the believing community.

16) How do these argue for a universality of this Renewal?

The Church's greatest need is to come totally under the Spirit. At Pentecost, since the entire community was gathered in the Upper Room, the entire Church was totally under the Spirit.

Today, that goal is reached differently. The Spirit's manifestations are once again abundant. These experiences and the Spirit's primacy are linked together. Faith in the Spirit leads to a seeking of His manifestations. That seeking leads to manifestations. Manifestations lead to increased faith.

Pentecostal teachings should lead to a total primacy of the Spirit over the believing community. If these teachings are set aside, then the Spirit's primacy will never occur.

(D) REASONS FROM PRACTICES AND EXPERIENCES

17) How do the practices and experiences in the Renewal point to universality?

The experiences of the Renewal, especially where there is adequate pastoral care, show that experiencing the Spirit is meant for all.

18) What has happened?

People involved in the Renewal

1) have experienced a conversion from darkness and a call to light. They each have a personal story of when and how this happened.

2) have experienced a beginning gift of prayer and the sense of God's protective presence.

3) pray in tongues.

4) have enjoyed religious experiences as an on-going gift.

19) Don't other believers, not involved in this Renewal, experience the same gifts?

Certainly, some Catholics not involved in the Renewal experience some of the above changes. However, the percentage of Catholics experiencing them is much greater in the Renewal.

Also, the Renewal is composed of average Catholics. Comparing their life before and after involvement in this Renewal would show that the Spirit is much more active within them after they entered the Renewal.

These average Catholics proclaiming the changes brought about in their lives are evidence that these same changes can and should occur in every Catholic's life.

20) What does the Renewal do to foster these experiences among its members?

The Renewal focuses upon and highlights these religious experiences.

21) What is the value of placing such stress on these experiences?

Valuing these experiences is important because:

1) When taught and sought, these experiences occur more frequently.

2) When seen as important, they are not put aside.

3) When received, they are better understood.

4) When understood, they are protected by correct teaching and guidance.

22) What is the value of these experiences happening more frequently?

Since the Early Church's fervor after Pentecost was filled with experiences of the Spirit, their renewed presence brings the modern Church closer to the scriptural ideal.

(E) BASIS IN SCRIPTURE

23) *Where does Scripture say that everyone should belong to the Pentecostal Renewal?*

This book doesn't claim that everyone should belong to the Pentecostal Renewal. It does teach that those powers currently abundant within the Renewal are for all.

24) *Where does Scripture say that these powers of this Renewal should be for all?*

A surprising number of New Testament quotes and contexts clearly teach a universality. This universality extends to both the Spirit Himself and to His charismatic actions.

25) *What Scriptural texts show the Spirit is a gift for all?*

The following show a clear universality:

1) After the Resurrection, Jesus bestowed His Spirit upon all.

> "Then He breathed on them and said:
> 'Receive the Holy Spirit'." (Jn 20:22)

2) In the Acts, the Spirit is always given to everyone present

    a) At the first Pentecost:

> "All were filled with the Holy Spirit." (2:4)

    b) After Peter's Pentecost address:

> "Those who accepted his message were baptized; some three thousand were added that day." (2:41)

c) Peter and John in Samaria:

"The pair upon arriving imposed hands on them and they received the Holy Spirit." (8:17)

d) Peter with the Gentile Cornelius and his family:

"...the Holy Spirit descended upon all who were listening to Peter's message." (10:44)

e) Paul at Ephesus:

"As Paul laid his hands on them, the Holy Spirit came down on them... There were in the company about twelve men in all." (19:6-7)

26) *Does St. Paul teach a universal outpouring?*

Paul's primary teaching was that the Spirit was for all believers.

1) "All of us have been given to drink of the one Spirit." (1 Cor 12:13)

2) "There is but one body and one Spirit, just as there is but one hope given all of you by your call." (Eph 4:4)

(F) UNIVERSAL INTERNAL ACTIONS

27) *Where does Jesus speak of the Spirit's action within every believer?*

Jesus' whole teaching on the Paraclete clearly promises the Spirit's universal presence and activity. He teaches:

1)   The Spirit's presence. (Jn 14:16)

2)   The Spirit instructing and reminding all. (Jn 14:26)

3)   The Spirit bearing a universal witness to Jesus. (Jn 15:26)

4)   The Spirit guiding all to truth. (Jn 16:13)

28) *Where does Paul teach a universality of the Spirit's actions within believers?*

1)   He expects all to be led by the Spirit.

"All who are led by the Spirit of God, are sons of God." (Rom 8:14)

2)   He expects the Spirit to pray within:

"You did not receive a spirit of slavery leading you back into fear, but a spirit of adoption through which we cry out, 'Abba!' (that is 'Father!')." (Rom 8:15)

3)   He proclaims a helplessness without the Spirit:

"And no one can say: 'Jesus is Lord' except in the Holy Spirit." (1 Cor 12:3)

4) He expects an internal change in every believer because of the Spirit's gift:

> "All of us gazing on the Lord's glory with unveiled faces, are being transformed from glory to glory into His very image by the Lord who is the Spirit." (2 Cor 3:18)

(G) UNIVERSAL CHARISMATIC ACTIVITY

29) *Where does Jesus speak of universal charismatic gifts?*

1) Jesus promises universal charismatic activity:

> "I solemnly assure you,
> the man who has faith in me
> will do the works I do,
> and greater far than these." (Jn 14:12)

2) Jesus promises a universal witnessing to the ends of the world:

> "You will receive power when the Holy Spirit comes down on you; then you are to be my witness in Jerusalem, throughout Judea and Samaria, yes, even to the ends of the earth." (Acts 1:8)

3) Jesus promises extraordinary signs accompanying belief. He begins this promise,

> "Signs like these will accompany those who have professed their faith..." (Mk 16:17)

Never does Jesus limit those who will enjoy the Spirit's charisms.

30) Do the Acts record universal charismatic activity?

The Acts of the Apostles records universal charismatic activity. Like Jesus, the Acts expect charisms to be used by all:

1) Among those gathered at Pentecost:

    "They...made bold proclamations as the Spirit prompted them." (2:4)

2) At the second surprise outpouring:

    "They were filled with the Holy Spirit and continued to speak God's word with confidence." (4:31)

3) At the Gentile outpouring:

    "...whom they could hear speaking in tongues and glorifying God." (10:46)

4) As Paul laid hands on the disciples at Ephesus:

    "...they began to speak in tongues and to utter prophecies." (19:6)

31) Where does Paul teach universal charismatic activity?

Paul's teaching is clear:

1) God's diverse works are in everyone:

    "There are different works but the same God who accomplishes all of them in everyone." (1 Cor 12:6)

2) All should contribute:

"To each person the manifestation of the Spirit is given for the common good." (1 Cor 12:7)

3) All can speak prophecies:

"You can all speak your prophecies, but one by one, so that all may be instructed and encouraged." (1 Cor 14:31)

4) All should seek charismatic activity:

a) "Set your hearts on the greater gifts." (1 Cor 12:31)

3) "Set your hearts on spiritual gifts—above all, the gift of prophecy." (1 Cor 14:1)

(H) IMPORTANCE

32) Why are these texts important?

They show that the Pentecostal Renewal fosters charisms and other actions of the Spirit which the New Testament expects every believer to manifest.

33) Why are these Spirit manifestations not universal in the Church today?

These powers were lost to the mainstream of Catholicism. Although devout people experienced some of these actions and the Church's theology taught they were valid religious experiences, they were not seen as universal.

34) Why is it important for the Church to see these Pentecostal gifts as universal?

To teach that these actions are valid and available for some is quite different than saying they should be experienced by all. Gifts available for some demand only a passive acceptance. Gifts for all demand active promoting and seeking. The Church's pastoral activity would change drastically if the charisms were seen as universally necessary.

(I) CONCLUSION

35) How do these questions touch upon the universality of the Pentecostal Renewal?

The questions highlight the following dilemma and contradicton:

1) The Pentecostal Renewal as now structured could never include every Catholic.

2) The powers of the Spirit upon which the Renewal is based should include every Catholic.

Universality is planted like a seed within this Renewal. How the full harvest will come about is still not clear.

Chapter 8
THE GOALS OF THE RENEWAL

A Renewal's beginning is marked by activity, sometimes feverish. Everything is new. People are excited. A structure has to be built, books written, and conferences set up.

No questions about goals are asked. The pressing demand for service and help push such questions aside. Inevitably, however, they have to emerge. When the beginning fervor wains, when the years pass and some perspective is available, the time comes to ask the question, "What is this Renewal all about?"

The question was always there, being answered in a hundred practical and partial ways. Yet, more is needed. Partial answers don't suffice. Practical answers can be misleading.

The same problem arose in the Early Church. After the beginning years of feverish missionary activity, the Apostolic Community had to face the questions of the Church's goal. The visionary was Paul, who claimed direct divine revelation. Paul, alone, was not enough. Others had to agree with him. When common understanding was reached, Christianity's basic truths were in place. The goal was clear and the Spirit's power could continue to spread.

The same process must happen within this Renewal. Only when the goal is clear can the Spirit's power continue to spread.

(A) OPINIONS ABOUT THE GOALS

1) What are the goals of this Renewal?

There is no consensus on the exact goals. All agree that certain aspects, as the Baptism of the Spirit, praying in tongues, and charisms are central elements. However, just where these are meant to lead is not clear.

2) What goals are agreed upon?

All agree that people should be touched by the Spirit, enter into religious experiences, persevere in using charisms and find their role in Christ's body. After that common ground, various questions arise about the purpose of this movement.

3) What are the important questions about these goals?

There are three major questions:

1) Is this Renewal meant for everyone?

2) Is a person meant to stay within the Renewal or meant to move into service in the wider Church or in the world?

3) If a person stays in the Renewal, what is meant to happen?

4) What opinions arise concerning these questions?

The following are the general categories of responses.

1) The Pentecostal Renewal is not meant for everyone, but represents one style of spirituality that appeals to some, and not to others. Therefore, the Renewal has not failed if many are not involved.

2) People are meant to be part of this Renewal for a while. However, the Renewal is like a novitiate in which people are spiritually changed but then are meant to move on to a life of service. People dropping out do not represent a failure at all but a normal process to be expected.

3) This Renewal is for everyone and people should not be dropping out. Therefore, if people have not been touched by this Renewal or have dropped out of active participation, then the Renewal is not fulfilling its goals.

5) What are the weaknesses of these opinions?

All three opinions have many weaknesses:

1) To say that this Renewal is meant for only a small number of Catholics fails to grasp the underlying theology. This opinion is based on a superficial understanding. Because relatively few Catholics identify with this Renewal, it is quickly declared as "only for some". Just as Catholic theology used to teach that speaking in tongues was only for the Early Church because this phenomena was not

present, so some claim that this Spirit's outpouring is only for some because all do not belong to this Renewal.

2) To say that people are meant to be touched by the Renewal and then move on to service in the Church or in the world gives the impression that the Pentecostal Renewal can only bring about a beginning religious experience.

If this Renewal is only a novitiate, then what is meant to provide full spiritual growth for a lifetime? This opinion willingly accepts the "status quo" of people dropping out without forcing charismatic leaders to search even deeper into the Spirit's designs.

3) To say that everyone should belong to this Renewal and no one should drop out does not take into account this Renewal's very frail structure.

6) *Should every Catholic be a member of this Renewal? Is it for some and not for others? Are people meant to move on to service in other areas?*

All these questions do not get to the central goal of this Renewal. These are secondary questions. Trying to answer them only increases confusion.

7) *What is the central question?*

The central question concerns a vision of the Church in which the Holy Spirit is totally active. The central question of this Renewal is, "How does God intend His Church to be renewed through this outpouring of the Spirit?" The goals are contained only in God's revealing to us His plan.

(B) GOD'S REVEALING IN SCRIPTURE

8) *Where does the New Testament speak of the Spirit revealing His goals?*

Paul constantly stated the importance of God's revealing gift.

1) He revealed the gospel to Paul.

> "I did not receive it from any man, nor was I schooled in it. It came by revelation from Jesus Christ." (Gal 1:12)

2) He revealed His plan.

> "No, what we utter is God's wisdom: a mysterious, a hidden wisdom. God planned it before all ages for our glory." (1 Cor 2:7)

3) He revealed His plan for the Gentiles.

> "I became a minister of this Church through the commission God gave me to preach among you His word in its fullness, that mystery hidden from ages and generations past but now revealed to his holy ones." (Col 1:25-26)

9) *Was it enough that Paul saw the goal?*

Not at all. The whole Church had to grasp this vision. This happened at the Council of Jerusalem.

"At that the whole assembly fell silent. They listened to Barnabas and Paul as the two described all the signs and wonders God had worked among the Gentiles through them." (Acts 15:12)

10) Why did the whole Church have to see these goals?

The Spirit could act fully only after the Church leaders recognized His actions. Otherwise, the Gentile missionary harvest would have split the Apostolic Community.

Fortunately, the leaders agreed on their goals.

"On the contrary, recognizing that I had been entrusted with the gospel for the uncircumcised,...and recognizing, too, the favor bestowed on me, those who were the acknowledged pillars, James, Cephas and John, gave Barnabas and me the handclasp of fellowship, signifying that we should go to the Gentiles as they to the Jews." (Gal 2:7-9)

11) What was the effect of Paul's seeing his goal?

He didn't spend his time on useless, secondary issues. Seeing what had to be done, Paul brought people to know Jesus Christ and experience the power of His Spirit.

In turn, those who were converted understood the same goals. They quickly went from hearing the Word to preaching the Word to others. The message they brought was clear and the gospel message spread.

12) What was the effect of the Church seeing the goal clearly?

The effect was Christianity itself, which has lasted 2,000 years, and has a clear message about the role of Jesus Christ and the power of His Spirit. These goals were revealed to Paul for the Church's good.

> "That is why to me, Paul, a prisoner of Jesus Christ on behalf of you Gentiles, God's secret plan as I have briefly described it was revealed." (Eph 3:3)

(C) PAUL AND THE RENEWAL

13) Why is this scriptural example important to the Pentecostal Renewal?

The goals of this Renewal are based upon Paul's vision. Paul did not found Christianity (although some accuse him of this). He did grasp by divine revelation, better and quicker than anyone else, what Christianity was all about. He also clung to that goal, through thick and thin, and probably went to his death because of his understanding.

14) What was Paul's vision?

Very simple. The Spirit was for everyone. If that truth were preached, then the power of Christ's resurrection would not be void. If it weren't preached, or if it were mixed in with other secondary, passing or outdated truths, then the people would miss out on the power of the New Age.

15) What, then, are the goals of Pentecostal Renewal?

The same as Paul's. The Spirit is for everyone. That truth must be grasped and preached clearly. In this sense, Pentecostal Renewal is for everyone.

16) Was this Paul's only message?

It was his basic message. His other teachings flowed from this. Much teaching dealt with growth in the Spirit's powers or misconceptions that ruined that power.

(D) SIMPLICITY OF THE GOAL

17) Isn't the goal that the Spirit is for everyone too simple to embrace the many aspects of Christianity?

The Spirit, as the soul of the Mystical Body, touches every part of the Church. A view of Christianity as just a collection of elements, all somehow linked together, fails to grasp the central mystery of Jesus reconciling all to the Father through His Spirit.

18) What is meant by a collection of elements?

A collection of elements is any theology that sees Christianity as a collection of dogmas, sacraments, commandments and devotional practices, without even grasping that all of these have the Spirit as their source. In fact, the Spirit Himself is seen as just one more dogma.

19) *How does this vision help to define the goals of the Pentecostal Renewal?*

This Renewal has primary and secondary goals. Seeing the Spirit as a universal gift defines the primary goal of the Renewal.

The secondary goals concern the Renewal itself. These include the spread of prayer groups and the growth of conferences. However, the primary goal goes beyond these secondary objectives.

20) *Why is the primary goal not contained in these secondary objectives?*

Because the Renewal does not exist for itself but for the Church, just as a seed exists only that the plant come forth.

(E)   THE DIVERSE ELEMENTS

21) *If this is the goal, how come the Pentecostal Renewal has so many diverse elements.*

Seeing that the Spirit is for everyone has led to these diverse elements. The Renewal, in trying to make the Spirit known, has gone in many directions.

22) *Do these diverse elements point to the goal?*

The Renewal itself can get lost in all of its own diverse elements and fail to realize that its true goal is making the Spirit available for everyone. It is important to see the Spirit as Jesus' first gift.

23) Why is this important?

Healing is not Jesus' first gift. Nor are prayer groups, or conferences, or even the Pentecostal Renewal itself. The Spirit is His first gift.

The Renewal's goal is that the Spirit be powerful in every person in this world. To say that this Renewal is supposed to help only some, is not true. To say the person should be initiated into the Spirit and then move on to other service, fails to see the Spirit's continuing role. To say that everyone is supposed to join a prayer group confuses the primary goal with what is only one element of this Renewal.

24) Is this "seeing the Spirit is for everyone" the goal of the Church or the goal of Pentecostal Renewal?

Both. It is the total goal of the Pentecostal Renewal. It is the central goal of the Church. The process of how the goals of a Church movement are accepted as the goals of the Church is treated in the chapter entitled, "The Church and the Renewal".

25) What is meant by the distinction between the "total goal of the Renewal" and the "central goal of the Church"?

This Renewal focuses on one central aspect, namely that the Spirit become the primary force in everyone's life. That was the focus of the Early Church. However, 2,000 years have passed and the Spirit has led the Church into many diverse areas. The Modern Church is not called to be the Early Church because that would repudiate 2,000 years of the Spirit's work.

However, these centuries have never changed the Church's central goal, which is exactly the same as the Pentecostal Renewal goal. The goal of having the Spirit active within every person is the total goal of the Renewal and the central goal of the Church.

26) Isn't Jesus Christ supposed to be everyone's Lord? Why is that not the central goal of the Church?

Having everyone confess that Jesus is Lord is the Spirit's goal. If the Holy Spirit is not active within the believer, then Jesus Christ is just a historical person who lived 2,000 years ago. Jesus becomes the believer's Lord only through the Spirit:

> "And no one can say: Jesus is Lord, except in the Holy Spirit." (1 Cor 12:3)

Chapter 9
DIFFICULTIES IN THE RENEWAL

This chapter highlights two sets of difficulties. The first concerns helping the individual become established in a new spiritual life. The second involves the Renewal itself, and primarily the problem of people dropping out. This is not meant to be a discouraging chapter, but a grasping of the central questions of what the Renewal can and cannot do.

Difficulties cause people to think, to analyze, and to ask questions. If that process wearies or debilitates, the effect is paralysis. If the questioning leads to answers, hope, and encouragement, then the Spirit of God is in the process. Difficulties and setbacks can be seen as unwanted problems or as roads leading to new doors for the Spirit's action.

Unbounded success, continuous growth and total overcoming of all difficulties seemed a very possible dream in the early years. For all of us who are deeply immersed in this Renewal, the fire of the New Pentecost has never disappointed, has never failed to provide, and has never resulted in the disappointment of the Emmaus disciples. The glory of God is that "Praise the Lord" remains on our lips even when difficulties crowd around our hearts.

(A) DIFFICULTIES WITH PERSONAL COOPERATION

1) With such an outpouring of the Spirit, why are there so many difficulties?

In no aspect of Catholic faith is personal cooperation so difficult. Even with the Spirit's initiatives and gifts, much is required from the person.

2) Why is much required?

The Spirit penetrates the person's deepest faculties and demands a complete yielding. This yielding is progressive. A partial commitment is not enough. The person must fully yield his life to Christ's Spirit. The greatest difficulty is the demand of personal cooperation required by the Spirit.

3) What other difficulty exists?

A second difficulty centers around the help and cooperation needed from others. The Spirit calls believers into the Body of Christ where relationships are meant to help and sustain. Everyone's growth in the Spirit depends upon others also growing in the Spirit.

4) Why are these relationships not always present?

Within the Renewal there is often a lack of pastoral care needed to bring people together. As a result, the Spirit's work comes undone, or never progresses beyond the initial step of personal conversion.

5) Are there other difficulties?

All the powers warring against God's Kingdom are also a threat to the Pentecostal Renewal of the Church. The more obvious and overpowering difficulties are:

1) The new powers of the modern world.

2) The total disarray of modern culture.

3) Misdirected economic systems.

4) Satan and his legions.

The list is endless. Since this Renewal tries to change people who live in the world, all these powers present difficulties.

(B) SOURCES OF DIFFICULTIES

6) What is the initial difficulty?

First, people must be led to search for a deeper Catholic life.

7) Why don't people search for this life?

Many have no idea that such a life exists or is available to them. Others are quite content with the present level of their religious practice. Still others have totally abandoned religion. These would be the three main groups that don't search for a life in the Spirit.

8) Has the Renewal been successful in inviting people to a life in the Spirit?

The Renewal itself is an invitation. Those attracted to the Renewal have experienced this door to a new life.

9) Has the Renewal been successful in bringing people to this deeper life?

In this area there has been true success. The Renewal has clear means—the teaching seminars, the laying on of hands, and the Spirit's gifts, to help people experience the initial conversion and prayerfulness.

10) What are the difficulties?

There are two difficulties:

1) In spite of what many consider widescale publicity and success, a relatively small percentage of Catholics actually participate in the Renewal.

2) More important, the follow-up and the perseverance in the initial conversion experience is weak.

(C) DIFFICULTIES IN PERSEVERANCE

11) What are the sources of this weakness in perseverance?

This weakness, the most important difficulty in the Renewal, has two main sources:

1) The goal itself seems impossible. Even religious and priests find difficulty in leading a strong daily life of prayer. The goal of this Renewal is that every

Catholic, even those deeply immersed in the world, lead a daily prayer life and commit themselves to a weekly period of communal prayer.

2) While experiencing the initial changes the person can easily see what has happened. They can contrast the before and after. Such evident signs are not present in the growth or follow-up stage.

12) Are there any other difficulties at this second stage?

Leaders don't know how to cope with this problem. Leading the person to conversion and religious experiences is clear. After the initial breakthrough, what the individual needs is not clear. At this point, leaders grow confused, not always knowing how to lead the people further.

13) Are there other difficulties which must be faced?

From the initial conversion experience until the person completely finds his/her basic role in the Renewal, many questions arise. The person must face the following:

1) How to pray daily.

2) How to put their life in order.

3) How to be of service to others.

4) How to yield to charisms.

5) With whom to be associated in this Renewal.

These five areas are interrelated and depend on one another. All five must be touched by the Spirit, or true growth will not happen.

(D) DIFFICULTIES IN THESE FIVE AREAS

14) What is expected in daily prayer?

Introduced into the unseen world of God's presence, the person cannot allow his/her time to be swallowed up by the world. The believer must deliberately find time to withdraw from that world to experience, again and again, the unseen world of God's Spirit. Given the pace and demands of the modern world, such a daily prayer time is extremely difficult to maintain.

15) Why must the person put his life in order?

The person's life must be put in order just as the hole in a bucket has to be fixed. Trying to fill such a bucket, without fixing the hole, is a waste of time.

16) Why must a person be of service to others?

The final aspect of the prayer gift is "to bring forth fruit." (Jn 15:16) After the person has experienced God, and reordered his/her life, there must be service to others.

17) Why must the person yield to charisms?

Modern theology correctly sees that the person's prayer life and their service to the Church are deeply intertwined. The charisms are the Spirit's powers equipping the person to serve. Without these charisms, either the person does not bother to serve or tries to serve by his/her own powers. Neither method contributes to growth.

Although the charisms are freely given gifts, the Spirit intends some charism for everyone. He does not envision a person who doesn't serve the community.

18) Why must the person be rooted in relationships?

The person, brought to the conversion experience through others, will only grow by remaining with people who are themselves committed to growth in the Spirit.

This is a very tricky and difficult question. Relationships, an indispensable means of growth, are at the same time filled with difficulties. Correct relationships with the right people will solve many difficulties and prevent new problems. The wrong relationships will ruin everything.

After years in the Renewal, it has become evident that a person with no relationships can not come to full growth in the Spirit.

19) Why are all these difficulties present?

This Renewal aims very high. It seeks a Catholic who prays daily, is committed to others in relationships, and serves the Church through powers given freely by the Spirit.

The Renewal demands a high degree of awareness and daily cooperation. Because each person is unique, these high goals can be brought about only through the Spirit.

20) Has the Renewal worked out adequate answers to these difficulties?

Although the Renewal's present answers are still inadequate, it has faced these difficulties.

(E) DIFFICULTIES WITHIN THE RENEWAL ITSELF

21) *What are the difficulties within the Renewal?*

Unlike the early years, a large number of newcomers no longer enter the Renewal. At the same time, fewer are leaving. Yet, even with both factors, the vitality of the early years seems to be missing. This has led many to experience doubts and discouragement.

22) *Are there other problems besides people not entering?*

There are many serious questions concerning any realistic hope of renewing the whole Church. The following seem to be the outstanding ones:

1) The Renewal does not attract men in the same degree as the Church does.

2) Very few priests actually participate on a regular basis.

3) The prayer group structure is very frail. This fragility was covered over by the enthusiasm and excitement of the early years.

4) Many individual prayer groups do not manifest the full charisms of the Spirit, nor do they offer the necessary pastoral care to foster permanent involvement.

23) *If people are not entering the Renewal and others are dropping out, how can there be any hope of this Renewal touching everyone?*

First, the Renewal itself was the Spirit's surprise. Having surprised us once, the Spirit can provide new directions and a new outpouring.

(F) DIFFICULTY OF DROPPING OUT

24) *What is the biggest difficulty of the Renewal?*

The largest difficulty concerns those who have dropped out. If all, or even a large percentage, were still active, the original vitality would very much exist.

25) *What of the opinion that people should only be in the Renewal for a period of time and then move on to other service?*

Many people are changed by their charismatic experience and offer help elsewhere. However, the Renewal offers a committed spirituality that seems to exist nowhere else. Therefore, dropping out most often means a lower level of prayer.

The opinion that people should move out of the Renewal into other services for the Church, although valid in some cases, cannot be readily applied to all.

26) **Does this dropping out represent a failure of the Renewal?**

Dropping out is more a weakness than a failure. Obviously, the prayer groups would have much more vitality if everyone stayed and remained active. However, looking at the Renewal, its goals and its present structure, dropping out seems inevitable.

(G)   REASONS FOR DROPPING OUT

27)   **What hastens or brings about "dropping out"?**

The following are basic reasons:

1)   Many prayer groups lack elements that would keep people coming.

2)   After the initial conversion experience, many do not know how to grow and see no need for a continued commitment.

3)   The motivated person must find a weekday time to be free of other duties.

28)   **Why is it difficult to keep people coming?**

Being a new member of the Renewal brings an excitement. Newcomers feel they have made spiritual progress, had their first religious experience and have begun praying in tongues. The real difficulty is to provide sufficient spiritual growth that will keep people returning for years.

29)   What is needed?

The prayer groups need two parts:

1)   Members who see the personal spiritual need for a weekly charismatic gathering.

2)   Leaders who can foster a high quality prayer meeting.

Obviously, both that quality of leadership and the needed commitment by members are difficult to come by.

30)   What is the difficulty with growth after the initial conversion experience?

The initial spiritual changes are obvious. People become discouraged when later spiritual growth is not as obvious nor so exhilarating. Also, leaders know how to give initial teachings and lay hands for the Baptism of the Spirit. They often don't know where to go from there.

Therefore, both leaders and members face the problem of growth after the initial months of charismatic involvement.

31)   What is the obstacle of a weekday time for this Renewal?

Possibly, this is the greatest problem causing charismatic "drop out". Americans put aside Sunday morning (or Saturday evening) for religious observance. The average Catholic parish offers a schedule of masses, so that every interested parishioner can participate. Even non-religious family members tend to cooperate, at least allowing the interested person to attend Church.

Once religious services of any kind move away from the Sunday morning (or Saturday evening) time frame, there are significant attendance problems. The pressures of the modern world and the demands of work and family, leave little time for large numbers to attend a weekly religious meeting.

Since charismatic groups are usually scheduled into a weekday night, their ability to attract large numbers on a regular basis is limited.

32) *Wouldn't the solution be to have a charismatic Sunday Mass for those interested in this Renewal?*

That might only be a surface solution. The deeper questions concern the universality of this Movement (whether this action is meant for all), and the changes which happen when the Spirit totally permeates Church life.

Since the Mass should celebrate what is happening every day in the parish, a charismatic Sunday Mass should manifest a charismatically renewed parish.

Chapter 10
CRITICISMS OF THE RENEWAL

This Renewal has difficulties from within and criticisms from without. How do others perceive this Renewal? Where do they see flaws or even serious problems? How justified are their remarks?

This chapter is written from the perspective of those questions. Some criticisms have no basis. Other criticisms are true. Some criticisms deal with only certain groups within this Renewal. At other times, the criticism is directed at everyone.

How others see us cannot be the norm for direction because the Renewal must follow the Spirit. However, outside criticism cannot be rashly brushed aside, as if coming from those not touched by the Spirit.

If the Renewal hopes to affect everyone, it must listen and respond effectively to its critics. Sometimes the response need only be verbal. At other times, some actions must be taken. Always there must be a sincere attempt to avoid practices which draw legitimate criticism.

Critics and criticism, legitimate or otherwise, purify a Renewal. They are not obstacles but helps to the Spirit's works.

(A) SOURCES OF CRITICISM

1) Where does criticism come from?

Criticism comes from many sides, from those close to the Renewal and from those who know little about it. Some criticism is based upon truly valid questions, and other flows from emotion or prejudice.

2) What attitude should be taken toward criticism?

The Renewal should not assume a "holier-than-thou" attitude, which would see all criticism as coming from "non-spiritual" sources.

Since this Renewal hopes to attract everyone, it must examine criticism and see the causes. However, accepting all criticism as valid would ruin the Renewal, making it changeable according to every critic's whim and fancy.

3) What are the main criticisms of the Renewal?

The following eleven points cover the main criticisms:

1) There is too much emphasis on tongues.

2) The Renewal is too Protestant.

3) The Renewal is based upon emotion and superficiality.

4) People misuse the gifts, especially healing and prophecy.

5) The Renewal is imbued with Fundamentalism.

6) The Renewal's theology is too right wing.

7) The people don't get involved with social justice.

8) The people are withdrawn from other Church concerns.

9) The Renewal attracts the emotionally insecure.

10) The Renewal causes people to leave the Church.

11) The Renewal does not accept a modern role of women.

The following questions will detail each criticism and try to reply.

(B)   EMPHASIS ON TONGUES

4)   *Does not this Renewal place too much emphasize on praying in tongues?*

It is difficult not to emphasize tongues, even though many might be turned off by this approach. From the Renewal's point of view, tongues are important, because:

1)   They are readily available, seemingly to all.

2)   They are a unique expression of communal praise and extremely important to the prayer meeting.

3) They are the primary door to the charisms.

4) Without prayer tongues, the whole Pentecostal Renewal would be weakened and collapse.

Any leader who grasps the important power involved in prayer tongues has a very difficult time putting tongues in a secondary position. People who say this Renewal places too much emphasis on tongues should receive sound teaching. If this doesn't convince them, then they should be ignored.

(C) TOO PROTESTANT

5) *What is meant by being too Protestant?*

Since the split in western Catholicism over 400 years ago, very distinct Christian cultures have resulted. Catholic tradition, worship and religious practices are quite different than those found in Protestant churches. The following would be a fair picture of what Catholics mean by being too Protestant.

1) Overstressing personal religious experiences.

2) Downplaying liturgy and sacraments.

3) Losing sight of the Communion of the Churches, and the unity brought about by hierarchy.

4) Giving little value to the role of tradition and official Church teaching.

5) Overlooking those biblical texts which stress the importance of Church.

6) Isn't the Renewal based on practices common to Pentecostal churches?

The Renewal stresses charisms which are highly prized by the Protestant Pentecostal Churches. Since many of these gifts are not manifested in Catholic life, the Renewal, in that aspect, is Protestant. However, the gifts are rooted in Catholic tradition. Their absence or "non-use" is not a true Catholic tradition.

7) Does the Renewal become too Protestant?

Becoming too Protestant is a serious problem when the Renewal imbibes Protestant theology that sometimes accompanies the charisms. Long term exposure to Protestant ministers or bible groups also present serious problems of religious identity to Catholic Pentecostals.

This long term exposure can lead people into denominational teachings and practices. The prayer group, so affected, can experience:

1) a loss of a clear Catholic identity.

2) an inability to affect other Catholics because of becoming too Protestant.

8) Are there not other problems in stressing these Pentecostal elements?

If the true, valid Catholic structure is not strong, or if the Church is ineffective in certain areas, then the Pentecostal approach can overwhelm Catholics. Before a worshipping parish or diocese can become fully Pentecostal, it must first be fully Catholic. Otherwise, this Renewal poses serious problems.

If hierarchy, pastoral office, liturgy, sacraments, and the theology surrounding these, are not clearly established in people's minds, then these Catholic elements will be swept away in the Pentecostal tide.

9) What are effective measures against this problem?

It might be too striking to say, but the Pentecostal Renewal in any diocese should not be in the hands of Church amateurs. The tremendous need is for the church professionals to get into this Renewal and to allow the Renewal to get into them. This is the only solution to the constant problem of this Renewal becoming too Protestant.

(D)   EMOTIONALISM AND SUPERFICIALITY

10)   Is this Renewal too superficial and emotional?

This can be a definite problem. For example, many people are attracted by a healing service, but fewer people willingly accept fidelity to a weekly prayer group. People enjoy the emotional highs of large charismatic gatherings, but not the burden of daily prayer time.

The healing services and the large rallies are important. However, when the emotion has passed and the thrill of gathering is gone, there has to be daily fidelity to the Spirit and the Church.

If emotional praise is all the Renewal offers, then sincere Catholics will see no reason to participate.

11) How does the Renewal overcome superficiality and bring about lasting results?

The following are four sources of lasting results:

1) The Renewal must be well-founded on the local level. The more local, the better. Therefore this Renewal is more effective in the diocese than on the national level. Even the diocese should have regional levels, which support parish groups. The parish group itself must be based upon the family structure.

2) The Renewal must seek its power in charisms not in emotions. These charisms should lead to fidelity to daily prayer, correct priorities in decisions and strengthening of family relationships.

3) The top leaders in a diocese must be chosen from above (by the bishop). The Renewal would then be accepting the Church's model of authority structure. When all leaders are chosen (or discerned) by peers, too much stress is placed upon charismatic personalities and the ability to attract crowds. This presents a constant temptation to superficiality.

4) This Renewal must accent teachings. People should have a classroom experience in learning about religious experiences, charisms and charismatic practices. Only in this way can the Renewal's theology penetrate and be absorbed. If this Renewal rejects the solid pastoral and teaching

practices adopted by the Catholic Church then it must inevitably fall back on superficiality and emotion.

(E) MISUSE OF GIFTS

12) *How are the gifts misused?*

When healings are announced that don't happen and when prophecies don't come true, then gifts are being misused in a serious way. The charisms are also misused when:

1) God's intervening activity is allowed to substitute for human initiative.

2) Intercessory prayer excuses from social charity.

3) Pious thoughts are used for prophecy.

4) Deliverance is overused and the human factors involved in personality problems are overlooked.

True charismatic stories abound in the Renewal. These offer encouragement and hope. However, outsiders often hear stories of misuse of gifts. These stories place obstacles to charismatic involvement. "Lead My People" (section B) provides teachings on the duties of charismatic leaders in preventing a misuse of gifts.

(F)   IMBUED WITH FUNDAMENTALISM

13)   *Just what is Fundamentalism?*

Originally, Fundamentalism was a movement based upon 12 volumes entitled "The Fundamentals: A Testimony to the Truth" (1905 to 1915). These books were a reaction to liberal theology that had infiltrated Protestant seminaries and universities.

Following those books, a Fundamentalist Movement was formed in 1919 which, for the next decade, sponsored annual rallies and regular publications. By 1930, the Movement had lost its effectiveness. However, the seeds of the modern Fundamentalist approach were sown deeply, especially within the Southern Baptist church.

14)   *What does Fundamentalism mean today?*

The word means a certain approach to Christianity which is narrow and not open to other viewpoints. The main characteristics are the following:

1) Lack of openness to a scientific approach to scripture.

2) Quoting scripture out of context to support a fundamental truth.

3) The setting aside of theological writings.

4) The total stress on the personal conversion experience.

5) The setting aside of psychology and other understanding of human behavior.

6) Stressing the Second Coming and those scripture texts which focus on divine judgment.

15) Is Fundamentalism a problem in the Renewal?

Since this Renewal stresses the Baptism of the Spirit, the importance of personal religious experiences, the daily use of scripture, the charisms, and the Lordship of Jesus, the falling into a Fundamentalist mentality is a constant temptation.

16) What can prevent such a problem?

First, people have to be taught to discern and to think. They should not be deceived by what appears to be a powerful stream fueled by the television preachers.

Secondly, contacts with Fundamentalist groups and preachers have to be severely limited.

Thirdly, people in the Renewal have to remain planted in the mainstream of their family and their Church. Their life cannot become totally absorbed by religion.

(G) A RIGHT-WING THEOLOGY

17) Is the theology of the Renewal right-wing?

Too often, the preaching and writing associated with this Renewal represents the theological right, sometimes, even the extreme right. Certainly, in the eyes of Catholic writers and publishers, Catholic Pentecostalism is seen as right wing.

18) Why is this so?

A number of reasons exist:

1) When Catholic Pentecostalism began (late 1960's) the leftward elements in the Catholic Church were extremely strong. Personalism, openness to all beliefs, criticisms of Church teaching and overthrowing of long-held truths were very powerful. Catholic Pentecostals discovered the power of liberation in the Spirit of Jesus. They also saw some destructive elements in progressive theology. Therefore, its teachings were originally an antidote against the extreme left.

2) The personal changes resulting from the initial conversion experience inevitably move a person to the right in moral teaching and practice.

3) The stress on the Bible often relegates intellectual work and theological speculation to a secondary place.

4) A tension always exists between individual holiness and communal justice. The former stresses personal sin while the latter focuses on social evil. Pentecostalism's first focus is personal holiness.

Given all of the above, this Renewal finds itself in the Church's theological right wing.

19) Is this good or bad?

Adopting a theology toward the right is an easier way of binding people together. Right wing theology provides clear and definite truths that all members can agree upon. In this theology, they experience a communal oneness. However, a theology to the right (or to the left) closes this Renewal's doors to the mainstream Catholic.

20)   What should be done?

This Renewal should not be identified with right-wing theology. There is no essential connection between this outpouring of the Spirit and any theology, right or left.

If the Church adopts pluralism, then the Renewal should try to see the wisdom in the Church's openness. Where pluralism is mistaken, there must be faith that the Spirit will purify the Church. The Renewal should not be a strident, right-wing voice against obvious defects resulting from the Church's openness.

(H)   LACK OF CONCERN FOR SOCIAL JUSTICE

21)   Is there any justification that the Pentecostal renewal is not involved with social justice?

The Renewal is not involved with many aspects of Church life, and should not be judged by outside goals.

The Catholic Church has a variety of goals. Renewal movements within the Church have more limited and more specific goals. Any Church movement should be acclaimed if it attains its goals and criticized if it does not. Harmful, evil or destructive goals could also be legitimately criticized.

22) *Should the Renewal be more involved in social justice issues?*

The Renewal is not the Church and represents just a small stream. Also, members should not be so involved in this Renewal that it absorbs their whole life. They should have time for other concerns including social justice.

Some leaders are calling for more social action involvement. This is legitimate. However, people need definite and fruitful forms for social action.

23) *Are members of the Renewal involved in social justice?*

As individuals, they are probably more sensitive to personal justice than the average Catholic. As a group, they are not deeply involved in social justice.

Social justice leadership itself seems to be a charism. As individuals or groups experience that gift of the Spirit, the Renewal will encourage it.

Charismatics tend to get deeply involved with their parishes. Probably, social action leadership should come from the parish and the diocese. Charismatics should and would be present to help.

(I) WITHDRAWAL FROM CHURCH CONCERNS

24) *Is not this Renewal withdrawn from other Church concerns?*

If the individual prayer group is turned in on itself, concerned only about its own growth and consuming too much of the members' time, then the people will be withdrawn from other Church concerns.

However, the Renewal teaches that members should be involved with their Church. In fact, charismatics actually fill many volunteer positions in a parish. This, certainly, is not withdrawal from Church concerns.

(J) LEAVING THE CHURCH

25) *Does not the Renewal cause people to leave the Church?*

In the early years, a resounding "no" could easily be given to this question. Just the opposite was true. Many Catholics returned to Church practice through Pentecostal involvement. Even today the Renewal continues to help Catholics return to the sacraments.

Over the years, some members of the Renewal have left the Church. Their reasons usually centered upon personal spiritual searchings that were not fulfilled in the Church's liturgical life. However, this loss of Church members is not limited to charismatics. All Catholics are being touched by the television preachers, the supposedly non-denominational bible studies and the outreaches of the aggressive Evangelical, Fundamentalist and Pentecostal wings of Protestantism.

26) *What can be done?*

Since the problem of leaving touches all types of Catholics, an adequate solution can come only from the Church. Preventing the problem requires the actions mentioned in many of these questions. By the time a person wants to leave the Church, the opportunity for preventive action has passed.

27) *What are the sources of this problem?*

Leaving the Church occurs with:

1)   Catholics who have little foundation in their own Church's teachings and are filling themselves with Pentecostal teaching.

2)   Renewal groups that downplay sacraments, especially the Sacrament of Reconcilliation.

3)   Leaders urging people to listen to or attend Protestant teachings without foreseeing the harmful effect.

(K)   ROLE OF WOMEN

28) *Does not the Renewal have strong ideas about the role of men and women which do not reflect modern thought?*

Many segments of the Renewal are not touched by this problem and the men-women relationships are no different than they are in the Church. Other groups have adopted strong teachings on the roles of men and women which would not reflect modern thought.

29) *Where do these teachings come from?*

Sometimes a group follows what they see as the biblical picture of male authority and female submission.

30) *What should be the picture of men-women relationships?*

Since the Spirit makes all things new, His actions should affect the relationship of men and women. When a man is touched by the Spirit, he should assume responsibilities in the home that he formerly refused to face. When a woman is touched by the Spirit, some aggression and hostility, usually associated with a liberated attitude, are removed. Also, the respect and thoughtfulness of the men toward women are heightened.

Obviously, both men and women touched by the Spirit adopt a much different attitude toward each other, but this cannot be criticized just because it doesn't correspond to the world's thinking. Generally, married couples touched by this Renewal are much happier than before.

Chapter 11
AUTHORITY
IN THE RENEWAL

People often think that authority and charisms don't mix. Supposedly, Pentecostalism should be Spirit-led, free and unburdened by authority structures.

Just the opposite is true. Before any group embarks on its charismatic journey, the question of who is in charge has to be answered. Otherwise, everything will be confusion. Charisms will not be discerned. Problems won't be adequately solved. People will grow frustrated and leave. All will be a shambles. Charisms need clear authority. Authority is needed at all three levels of the local prayer group, the diocese and the national level. Unfortunately, authority within this Renewal is not clear. Prayer groups use different methods of choosing leaders. Diocesan models vary greatly and so much depends on the local situation.

Covenant communities sometimes muddy the waters, having a great influence on the prayer groups but not having any diocesan authority. The national leadership also presents a confusing picture. No American bishop has authority over the Renewal. The various national groups are split and no one enjoys the authority needed to have true unity.

Authority is not a secondary question, able to be pushed into the background or solved by a common consensus. After all these years, the authority on every level, should be clear. However, it isn't. Opportunities are slipping away. The Renewal is losing ground. Activities take place that are at odds with other events. Efforts are duplicated and people are asked for money by anyone who feels led by the Lord.

The Renewal is helpless to put its own house in order unless it borrows the authority gift from the Catholic Church, which has always possessed the charism of unity through hierarchy.

A) AUTHORITY WITHIN THE MOVEMENT

1) Is authority clearly taught?

The Renewal has clear teaching on authority, both its necessity and the need for members to be obediently subject to lawful authority. However, many authority issues are not clear, still unanswered or not examined.

2) What is the model of authority within the Renewal?

Unfortunately, there is no clear model. It is not clear how people get their authority, or to whom leaders themselves are subject.

This lack of clarity even exists on the diocesan level. Often no single person has full authority within the diocesan renewal. The usual diocesan model involves a steering committee. How that diocesan committee gains its authority, or what authority the committee has over prayer groups is not clear. These committees use the word "service" to define their role but whether they are serving or commanding is not clear.

3) What is the picture of authority on the national level?

In the United States, the picture is confusing. No single person heads the Renewal. Various groups claim national prominence, but no one person or one group has any real authority that requires obedience.

Unfortunately, the confused American Renewal is often used as a model for other countries.

B) IMPORTANCE OF AUTHORITY

4) Why is authority so important in the Renewal?

People exercising charisms feel they are led by the Lord. These charismatic initiatives are important but need discernment. Without clear authority no one has the office to discern nor the power to correct. This results in people claiming a God-given ministry without anyone to effectively challenge that claim.

5) Why is authority important within the prayer group?

This Renewal urges people to accept a weekly committal to communal prayer. A group without clear authority is vulnerable to unaddressed problems, and to a complete inability to correct abuses.

People gathering weekly have a right to know who is in charge and how that person obtained authority. They also have a right to complain to a higher authority if leadership is poorly exercised.

6)   *How does a person get authority within a prayer group?*

The usual means are:

1)   the person is among those who began the group.

2)   the person was seen as the best leader when the original leader stepped down.

3)   the person was named by an outside authority, such as the pastor.

7)   *Which is the best means of naming a leader?*

The means varies. The means used to name someone is not as important as having the correct person chosen. Even more important is that authority over prayer group leaders is exercised by the diocesan authority.

8)   *Besides clear authority within the group why must there be a clear outside authority over prayer group leaders?*

First, discerning the prayer group leader is not always easy. Sometimes the group itself is divided over who should lead. In these cases, the outside authority helps or actually makes the decision.

Secondly, even a prayer group with a definite leader can be incorrectly led. The members must have a higher authority who can listen to their complaints and make a binding decision, even if it means the removal of that leader.

Thirdly, the leadership and the members might be doing things that are harmful to the other prayer groups, or to the Renewal within the diocese. A clear diocesan authority is needed to correct those problems.

C) DIOCESAN AUTHORITY

9) *Does this clear authority exist within the diocesan Renewal?*

The Renewal authority structure varies among dioceses. In some dioceses people don't see the need for clear authority. In other dioceses, they see the need but are helpless to bring it about.

10) *Why is there so much confusion concerning authority on the diocesan level?*

There has never been any clear teaching. The issue has been avoided. In 1976, the local bishops were asked to name diocesan liaisons to the Renewal. Liaison is not a clear word and is definitely not an authoritative word.

In Philadelphia, a very clear authority exists because Cardinal Krol saw that Diocesan Liaison was not a sufficient title. He named an Episcopal Vicar for the prayer groups. In Canon Law, an Episcopal Vicar enjoys all the powers of the bishop for the particular group he heads.

11) *Are people in the Renewal afraid of authority?*

When there is a clear authority there is always the possibility that the wrong personality would wield that power. However, such a fear would logically not want the Church to have bishops.

12) What are the alternatives to a clear diocesan authority?

Without a clear diocesan authority, the Renewal either evolves its own authority structures or moves along with no higher authority over the prayer groups and prayer communities.

13) What problems exist with a gradual evolving of diocesan authority?

A number of problems can exist:

1) The process can be manipulated by strong personalities.

2) The process can be cumbersome with people quarreling over the process itself (such as elections or delegates or terms of office).

3) The result of the process can be a limited, political type of authority that is fragile and unable to make difficult decisions that often have to be made.

4) In the course of the process, many people can just grow tired and drop out of the Renewal from frustration.

5) If a process is good and works, there is no guarantee that someone who doesn't like the process won't come along and want to change it.

14) What should be done concerning diocesan authority?

Some evolving is needed so leadership qualities can be proven and tested. The dangers of leaders being named only by a process can be remedied by using the authority of the Church.

This means that the bishop knows the people in the Renewal and correctly appoints the diocesan leader. He also must give that leader the true authority needed to make binding decisions and require accountability from that leader.

15) What are the problems with no diocesan authority, leaving authority matters to the local groups?

Many problems exist with this:

1) When the local prayer group experiences problems, no higher authority exists to help or to correct. Individual prayer groups are then totally helpless.

2) Many local prayer groups have poor leadership and are very poor models of this Renewal. A higher authority can at least see that the proper persons are leading the group.

3) Without diocesan authority, unity among the prayer groups depends totally on individual good will. Without higher authority, the prayer groups split, and go in various directions. This presents a scandal, rather than a divine sign, to those outside the Renewal.

16) Why is authority such an important issue?

Some authority is needed wherever large groups of people hope to stay united for a common goal. However, strong authority is especially needed in this Renewal because:

1) The Renewal fosters and trusts in the Spirit's initiatives within the person. This is dangerous unless it is clear what authority is discerning those promptings.

2) Since charisms involve human cooperation, even the greatest charismatic personalities can make gigantic mistakes. The greater the charism the more it must be subject to authority.

3) Charisms do not carry within themselves the gift of unity. If anything, their history shows they breed division. Clear authority is especially needed for those moments when charisms threaten to divide the Church or the Renewal.

17) Why do charisms divide?

Charisms have great power including the ability to attract large crowds. However, unlike Church office, charisms come directly from the Spirit to the person. Bestowed independently of Church authority, they are a second power within the Church. If authority is weak and charisms are strong, charisms can obliterate authority; just as strong authority, wrongly used, can destroy charisms.

Many churches with weak authority structures, condemn charismatic activity because they have seen the effects of these divisions. The American Catholic Church has been open to this Renewal because its authority is secure.

E) NATIONAL AUTHORITY

18) What is meant by a national authority?

National authority means the power to bring about compliance to the policies and decision of the authoritative person. It means that decisions are binding and effective whether those under authority agree with the reasons or not.

19) What is the state of authority on the national level of this Renewal?

No individual person is the national head of this Renewal. In fact, no authority that requires obedience exists on the national level.

As a result, anyone who feels led by the Lord can initiate any project or activity that they wish.

20) Is this adequate?

It is obviously very poor and very inadequate. Abuses cannot be corrected. National leaders themselves are divided. A duplication of effort, including the need to collect funds for undertakings has resulted.

21) Was there ever a true head of this Renewal on the national level?

There was never such a person nor has that idea ever been put forth. Cardinal Suenens received a mandate of pastoral care for the worldwide Renewal from Pope Paul IV and Pope John Paul II.

22) Why is there no individual person heading this Renewal?

The reasons are not exactly clear because the idea has never been discussed or brought up. Possibly, there is a fear that someone exercising clear authority would curtail what others wanted to do.

23) What is the solution to this dilemma?

This Renewal has to borrow the gift of authority and unity from the Catholic Church, which preeminently possesses this charism of unity.

This Renewal should ask the American bishops to name someone with full authority over the American Renewal.

24) Why is this important?

This Renewal cannot solve its own authority problems. Its structure is inadequate and is extremely vulnerable to divisions and splinter groups. Without authority, people and groups move in any direction they please.

It is especially important if this Renewal is to enter the Church's mainstream.

25) *Why is clear authority needed to bring this Renewal into the mainstream?*

First, American Catholics are used to clear authority. They will not accept a Renewal that has no one in charge.

Second, incorporation of the Renewal's gifts into the Church's life demands that the Renewal come more clearly under the bishops. On the diocesan level, the Renewal is under the bishop. On the national level, the Renewal is under no one.

Thirdly, clear national authority would allow the Renewal to move head in a united way.

Fourthly, before this Renewal can present itself for widescale acceptance by the average Catholic, it has to get its own house in order.

Section Three
The Renewal and The Church

Chapter 12
THE CHURCH AND
THE RENEWAL

Church history abounds with all kinds of movements, —some intellectual, others pietistic; some orthodox, others errant; some guided by saints, others by troublemakers. At a critical juncture, the Church decides what relationship to assume toward each movement. Heretical movements are condemned. Sanctifying ones are incorporated. A history of Church movement shows that some opportunities were grasped and others were lost. This chapter deals with the importance of the relationship of the Church to the Pentecostal Renewal, especially the incorporation of this Renewal into the Church.

At present, that incorporation is very partial. The Church has accepted this Renewal as valid. Catholics are permitted to participate. The Renewal aligns itself with the Catholic teachings and practices. Such a partial relationship will also be ineffective. If nothing changes, then the Pentecostal gifts will again die out and become marginal. Pentecostal groups will continue to exist, but for the most part the Renewal will decrease. Charisms planted only in the Renewal's soil have insufficient roots to last.

This chapter seeks a new relationship of the Church to the Pentecostal Renewal. Leaders in both have to grasp the importance of a closer, more integrated incorporation than now exists. The present stage is very temporary. Either the new Pentecostal flame will light up the Church or it will be blown out.

A) THE PENTECOSTAL RENEWAL OF THE CATHOLIC CHURCH

1) Would Catholics be open to a Pentecostal Renewal of the Church?

There are millions of wonderful Catholics who faithfully attend Church and who would be open to a Pentecostal Renewal that was clearly explained and properly guided. These Catholics have accepted other church renewals and are open to whatever is preached by the official Church.

2) What would the official Church be preaching?

The Church would be preaching personal religious experiences and the actions of the Spirit within each believer. This would include conversion experience, on-going religious experiences, charisms and communal prayers.

3) Why have they not been invited to these already?

Many have not been invited to these actions of the Spirit because they are seen as optional and secondary practices.

B) PRIMARY AND SECONDARY PRACTICES

4) *What are examples of primary and secondary practices?*

Receiving Holy Communion is a primary practice. Saying the rosary is secondary. Primary means that the practice is essential and every Catholic should participate. Secondary means the practice is optional and not every Catholic must be involved.

5) *Aren't secondary practices supposed to develop in movements within the Church, rather than as part of mainstream Catholicism?*

Secondary practices do belong in a movement. If the conversion experience, religious experience and charisms are secondary and optional, then they properly belong to a movement. If, however, they constitute primary practices then they are for the whole Church.

6) *Who decides what practices are primary and what are secondary?*

In the Catholic Church the hierarchy makes that decision. They base their decision upon a theological and pastoral reflection on what is actually happening.

C) THE LITURGICAL RENEWAL

7) *Is there a modern day example?*

At the Vatican Council the bishops examined various movements and decided that some elements should become Church practice.

The Liturgical Renewal is the outstanding example. While relatively few Catholics personally participated in the Liturgical Renewal Movement, all Catholics now share in its practices because the hierarchy saw the importance of these practices.

8) Did the bishops at Vatican II accept any other movements?

At the time of the Council, movements were flourishing in Ecumenism, Scripture and Theology. Many practices from these movements were accepted by the bishops.

9) What was the value of the bishops' decisions at the Council?

The council quickened the pace of acceptance. The powers of these movement entered directly into the Church's practices.

10) What can be learned from this?

Examining these movements and their later acceptance by the bishops shows the following:

1) A movement should focus upon and develop its own particular gifts.

2) During this initial period, the gifts mature.

3) A movement, no matter how large, will touch only a small percentage of Catholics.

4) The next step occurs when the hierarchy accepts the gift as a primary part of Church life.

5) With that decision, the gifts of the movement are placed in the bishops' hands.

6) This shift, however, does not guarantee results. The bishops' acceptance only provides a new opportunity for those gifts.

11) *Have the other movements enjoyed the same success as the Liturgical Renewal?*

A comparison between the Liturgical Renewal and the Ecumenical Movement show quite different fruits. Although the bishops fully accepted ecumenical goals and urged practices to unite the Churches, ecumenism is not currently flourishing.

12) *Why are the results quite different?*

Acceptance by the bishops does not automatically guarantee results. It merely provides for a new opportunity.

D) THE PENTECOSTAL RENEWAL

13) *At what stage of this process is the Catholic Pentecostal Renewal?*

This Renewal has already taken the first three steps. It has:

1) focused on its own particular gifts.

2) Used this time to mature.

3) attracted a percentage of Catholics.

14) *Have the powers and goals of the Pentecostal Renewal been accepted into the Church's mainstream?*

This step has not yet occurred. Various bishops' statements have spoken favorably of this Renewal. The bishops have not said that the Pentecostal gifts are primary.

15) *What is the difference between speaking favorably of religious experiences and seeing them as primary?*

Accepting religious experiences as primary would mean that they were important goals of the diocese. Priests would see these powers as normal practices of parish life. The Pentecostal Renewal would cease existing in its own little stream and be poured out into the Church's mainstream.

E) A FULL INCORPORATION

16) *What would happen if the bishops took that step?*

They would then commit the Church to fostering religious experiences within each Catholic and within each Catholic assembly.

17) *What would happen to the Church?*

If the acceptance were not followed by action very little would happen. The commitment would just remain on paper with little change in the Church's life.

If there were a full commitment and a follow-through, then the dream of "a new Pentecost in our day" would come true.

18) Should the bishops make such a commitment?

In God's plan, there is always the right moment. If Pope Pius XII had called an ecumenical council, the time and the situation would not have been correct and the results would have been minimal.

19) What should be done to bring about the correct situation and time?

That burden rests with the Pentecostal Renewal. For the time being the gifts have been placed within the Renewal. The duty of the Renewal is to mature and let the Church see the fruits of these Pentecostal powers.

20) Before taking this step what must the bishops see?

They would have to see that religious experiences should become as central to the Church as liturgical experiences. They would have to believe that the problems involved with these gifts would be worth the risk. They would also have to see that the Church is strong enough in other areas to handle this committal to Pentecostal experiences.

21) Why must the Church be strong enough in other areas before making a commitment to Pentecostal experiences?

Pentecostal experiences, both individual and communal, are not the only powers in the Church. The fullness of Catholic powers include sacraments, dogma, moral teaching and hierarchy. Pentecostal experiences can overwhelm these other elements. Sacraments can be put aside. Hierarchy can be bypassed by those who think they have a direct line to God. Some, in the exuberance of the Spirit, might feel the Church is too lax.

People must be well formed in the traditional powers and practices of the Catholic Church before Pentecostal experiences are totally accepted.

F)   AFTER THE COMMITTAL

22)   *What would insure a follow-through?*

The full value of Vatican II was not just a committal to changes, but that the bishops made that committal themselves. Through the communal experience of the Vatican Council, the bishops became dedicated to the goals they had set. This worldwide committal was insured by debates and discussion which preceeded the decisions.

23)   *Would a Pentecostal renewed Church depend on another ecumenical council?*

It would certainly depend on wide-scale teaching and discussion among the bishops. At first, these discussions should take place at the Bishops' Conference level. Later, the issues could be discussed at a Bishops' Synod in Rome.

Chapter 13
THE CHURCH AND CHARISMS

A problem (or opportunity) has to be faced. Within this Renewal people manifest charisms which are not used by the Church itself. A quick review of Paul's classical list (1 Cor. 12:7-11) shows that few of the nine charisms mentioned are known or practiced by the average Catholic. Specifically, tongues and interpretation of tongues are poorly understood even by the scriptural experts. The other seven gifts, while somewhat known, are little practiced.

The contrast is somewhat stark between one Church group knowing and using all of Paul's charisms, and another Church group not even acquainted with the list.

Some would say that charisms flourished at Corinth but not everywhere, and the Church should not be committed to one particular scriptural model. The gospels, however, are filled with Jesus' charisms. He shares those powers with the disciples and promises that "signs like these will accompany those who have professed their faith." (Mk. 16:17). Also the Acts record the Pentecostal charisms with a stress on the "many wonders and signs" that "were performed by the apostles." (2:43)

Vatican II, due to an important intervention of Cardinal Suenens, stated, "These charisms whether they be the more outstanding or the more simple and widely diffused, are to be received with thanksgiving and consolation for they are perfectly suited to and useful for the needs of the Church." (Constitution on the Church, Para. 12).

That statement opened the door to the Catholic Pentecostal Renewal. Whether it opened the door to a Church in which all the charisms flourish again is still to be seen.

A) UNDERSTANDING CHARISMS

1) What are charisms?

They are a special group of religious experiences. Besides being God's action within the person, they also serve another person or group.

Religious experiences, therefore, are either sanctifying or charismatic. The sanctifying experiences are for the good of the person being touched by God. A charismatic religious experience primarily serves another.

2) What are examples of both groups?

Sanctifying religious experiences include prayer gifts, personal peace or light for a decision. They are the many personal ways God protects and guides the individual.

Charismatic religious experiences include prophecy, healing, anointed preaching, reading of hearts, and many others. They are the regular ways God helps someone through another.

3) Is there a difference between ordinary and extraordinary charisms?

The Vatican council mentions that distinction (Constitution on the Church, Para. 12). However, the Council did not define the difference.

Some charisms listed in Scripture are seemingly natural talents, such as teaching, administrating or giving alms. Others are obviously beyond natural abilities, such as tongues, prophecy, healing or revealed knowledge.

4) Is the distinction important?

The Council seems to be concerned about a dangerous seeking after extraordinary gifts. The purpose of the Pentecostal Renewal is that all charisms, ordinary and extraordinary, be fully operative in the Church.

B) THE CHURCH AND CHARISMS

5) What has been the Church's attitude toward charisms?

That has varied over the centuries. Since these powers were the signs of Jesus' sending the Spirit, the Early Church welcomed and expected these outpourings. As time went on, this faith seemed to grow less. Problems concerning their use caused the Church to turn away from these gifts. Vatican II's statement signaled a renewed committal to fostering these gifts.

6) Are charisms important to the Church?

All would admit their importance, although opinions would vary over how important they are. Really, charisms are the Spirit's regular means of sanctifying. They are not optional powers which the Church can accept or forego. Without the charisms in full use, the Church's power is limited.

7)   What happens when the Church is limited?

Severe problems begin. People fall away and do not persevere. Instead of coming under the Spirit's powers, they are overcome by the world, by their own problems, by addictions or by the Kingdom of Darkness.

Problems also result within the Church. Just as a poorly nourished body grows weak, so the Body of Christ without the charisms is severely weakened.

C)   FOSTERING CHARISMS

8)   How do charisms become abundant again?

The first step is a deliberate fostering of religious experiences. Since charisms are a special class of these experiences, they will begin appearing as the people's inner life with God flourishes.

9)   Is it enough just to foster religious experiences?

Even when these experiences are abundant, charisms can be missing if they are deliberately excluded or not directly sought.

10)   How are charisms deliberately excluded?

This can happen directly or indirectly. If decisions are made that charism are not allowed, then they are being directly excluded. More often, the exclusion is indirect.

11) How are charisms indirectly excluded?

Indirect exclusion comes about in many ways:

1) the need for charisms is not seen.

2) the Church is content with its present powers and gifts.

3) the charisms are unknown or ignored.

4) No openness to charismatic manifestations exist.

12) What is the result?

The result of both direct and indirect exclusion is the same. Charisms do not flourish and God's power in the Church is limited.

13) Why must charisms be actively sought?

Charisms do not just pour out automatically and haphazardly to people who are totally passive in receiving them.

They are religious experiences, requiring like all religious experiences a human cooperation. Just as God blesses those who seek prayer gifts, so the Spirit is poured out upon those seeking His signs and wonders.

14) Why do some people seek charisms and others don't?

Some have experienced charisms and others haven't. Some see the Church's tremendous need for them and others think the Church can do all right without them.

15) How does the Church foster charisms?

The **first** step is to realize the absolute powerlessness of merely human activity (no matter how well thought out or how well financed) to build up the Body of Jesus Christ.

The **second** step is to believe that the Spirit's powers can restore the Church.

The **third** step is to seek, to know and to use all of the charisms.

(D) ATTITUDE OF THE CHURCH

16) Is the Church seeking these charisms?

Officially and theoretically, the Church wants the charismatic gifts present in the community. The question is the degree of seeking the charisms and the intensity of wanting them.

If the Church saw charisms as the answer to its present problems, there would be a total commitment to restoring them. Currently the Church doesn't have that degree of enthusiasm for charismatic gifts.

17) Should the Church make a total commitment to restoring charisms?

Again, the commitment to charisms is connected with the importance of religious experiences. Charisms are the final phase of religious experiences. Through charisms God moves people into service for others. The Church has stressed that every Catholic is called to service. By charisms, the Spirit provides the tools for service. It is useless to send people to serve unless they are equipped with powers.

18) **Isn't it wrong for the Church to focus on extraordinary charisms and set aside the ordinary means of service?**

This chapter is not based upon the distinction between ordinary and extraordinary charisms. It deliberately treats all charisms as important.

When, however, the so-called extraordinary charisms are excluded directly or indirectly, then even the ordinary charisms wane and grow frail. The final result is the substitution of human actions for the Spirit's power and directions.

(E) SCRIPTURAL BASIS

19) *What is the scriptural picture of charisms?*

Charisms are noticeably more present in the New Testament than in the Old. In fact, the universality of charismatic experiences is the sign of the Messianic Age. Sons and daughters, young men and old, even servants and handmaids will receive a portion of the Spirit and shall prophesy. These are the signs that "shall come to pass in the last days." (Acts 2:17-18)

20) *Where are charisms specifically present?*

In the gospels, Jesus' ministry is filled with charisms. He also confers upon the disciples the charisms of proclaiming the Kingdom, raising the dead, healing and casting out devils. (Mt. 10:7-8) He later commands them to use the charism of teaching (Mt. 28:20), and promises charisms as signs of belief. (Mk. 16:17-18).

In the Acts, the post-Pentecost Church manifests signs of tongues, as well as a full panoply of all the gifts. Both Peter and Paul raise people from the dead (Acts 9:40 and 20:7-12) and bring about widespread healings (Acts 5:12-16 and 19:11).

In the New Testament Letters, 1 Cor (C 12 and 14) contains the lengthiest and most complete description of charism. Romans (12:18) and Ephesians (4:11) also provide charismatic lists. The entire book of Revelation is a prophetic vision. Other books mention or praise charisms (2 Pt. and 1 Tim.)

21) What was Paul's teaching on charisms?

In 1 Cor. Paul's attitude concerning charisms is clear.

1) He wanted the charisms to be known.

   "Now, brothers, I do not want to leave you in ignorance about spiritual gifts." (12:1)

2) He wanted the people to seek charismatic activity.

   "Set your hearts on spiritual gifts — above all, the gift of prophecy." (14:1)

3) He wanted the Church to profit from the more powerful gifts.

   "You, then, are the body of Christ. Every one of you is a member of it. Set your hearts on the greater gifts." (12:27 and 31)

4) He did not want the charisms to be set aside.

"Set your hearts on prophecy, my brothers, and do not forbid those who speak in tongues." (14:39)

5) He expected charisms to be subject to church authority.

"…make sure that everything is done properly and in order." (14:40)

22) Did charisms extend only to extraordinary happenings?

We tend to think of extraordinary charisms, but the New Testament presents a clear picture of varied activities, both ordinary and extraordinary, attributed to the Spirit's intervention.

23) What would be some of the ordinary actions of the spirit?

Ordinary actions of the Spirit would be:

1) leading Jesus into the desert. (Mt. 4:1)

2) giving the disciples the correct words in difficult situations. (Mk. 13:11)

3) inspiring Simeon to come to the temple. (Lk. 2:28)

4) giving Peter the needed explanation of the Pentecost phenomenon. (Acts 4:8)

5) directing Philip's missionary activity. (Acts 8:29)

6) consoling the Church. (Acts 9:31)

7) filling the disciples with joy. (Acts 13:52)

8) guiding the decisions of the Jerusalem Council. (Acts 15:28)

9) preventing Paul from preaching to the wrong people. (Acts 16:6-7)

10) freeing believers from addictions. (Romans 8:2)

11) overcoming the power of sin. (Rom. 8:13)

12) bestowing a belief in God's Fatherhood. (Rom. 8:15)

13) helping believers to pray. (Rom. 8:26)

14) enabling people to live in harmony. (Rom. 15:5)

15) giving power to the preacher. (Thes. 1:5 and 1 Pt. 1:12)

16) preparing believers for future trials. (1 Tim 4:1)

24) Will not some of these activities go on without the presence of extraordinary charisms?

When a group does not seek all of the Spirit's charismatic activity, then even the ordinary manifestations seem to wane. To deliberately set aside some charismatic gifts threatens all of the Spirit's actions. This is how He became the forgotten Person of the Trinity.

25) What is the scriptural ideal?

Scripture says clearly that God should be in charge and that the Church should act in God's way and in God's power. This would mean:

1) An openness to all charisms

2) The actual use of all charisms in the community.

3) Through the charisms, the Church coming under God's sovereignity.

(F) PRESENCE OF CHARISMS

26) Does the Church have an openness to charisms?

By the statements of Vatican II and by the many statements of episcopal conferences concerning the Pentecostal Renewal, there certainly is a theoretical openness to the Spirit's charisms. Belief in healings, prophecies and miracles is not condemned as heretical. However, a charismatic flourishing demands an openness that seeks, asks and welcomes.

27) Are the charisms present and in use within the Church?

Although the official Church is open to charisms, many manifestations of the Spirit are weak or totally absent.

28) Why are they weak or absent altogether?

Charisms are weak and absent because they

1) are difficult to foster

2) cause problems

3) require a high level of faith

4) demand a purity of heart

5) are quick to die out

Charisms are like children. They bring endless problems, need constant surveillance and yet are the future hope of the Church.

(G) DIFFICULTIES WITH CHARISMS

29) *Why are charisms difficult to foster?*

Charisms are very special religious experiences that require daily human cooperation. They also require sanctity of life. Even though charisms are not signs of holiness, they flourish in people who are trying to be holy. A Church community seeking charisms also has to be seeking holiness. Holiness and charismatic manifestations are the most demanding aspects of the Christian life.

30) *Why do charisms cause problems?*

Charisms are dynamic and powerful. These powerful manifestations can lead many astray. Jesus said, "False messiahs and false prophets will appear, performing signs and wonders so great as to mislead even the chosen if that were possible." (Mt. 24:24)

A Church seeking powerful charisms will have to cope with the problems that always surround such gifts.

31) *Why do charisms require a high level of faith?*

Charisms are God's signs and wonders. They are not within a human being's power. They cannot be brought about "by man's willing it." (John 1:13). Greater faith is needed to discern and follow God's leadings then to try to do God's works from human motives. Since charisms are God's works, they demand an expectant and waiting faith.

32) Isn't this level of faith extremely difficult to attain?

Charisms bring about faith. People seeing and experiencing God acting, receive a faith increase. The initial faith in charisms increases as God acts and intervenes.

The same process also happens in reverse. Little faith in charisms stifles God's intervention. An absence of God's intervening convinces everyone that God really doesn't intend to intervene.

33) Why do charisms demand a purity of heart?

Charisms are God's actions within a cooperating person. They are always a mixture of divine and human activity. As John the Baptist said: "He must increase, while I must decrease." (Jn. 3:30)

The human, while always present, must give way more and more to God's action. Only with this purity of heart can the human person be lifted to the heights of being God's instrument.

34) Isn't this level of purity of heart limited to the saints?

The charisms themselves can bestow this needed purity of heart. People used as God's instrument see only too clearly their own frailty. By loving the people whom they are serving, charismatic persons become purified instruments.

35) Why are charisms so quick to die out?

They die out quickly because they demand this high level of human cooperation. Although charisms constantly die out, God continually renews His gifts. This modern Pentecostal Renewal is His latest attempt.

(H) THE SPREADING OF CHARISMS

36) Isn't it a dream to think that the extraordinary charisms will ever be fully restored to the Church?

Not at all. Experiences in the Renewal show that supposedly extraordinary charisms are quite available to all. Some charisms, such as celibacy, are obviously limited to some. However, tongues, intepretation, prophecy or any other charisms that could be called "extraordinary" are totally available through the Spirit who distributes them "to each as He wills." (1 Cor. 12:11)

37) How will the extraordinary charisms become present everywhere in the Church?

This will happen through

1) the mass media

2) the Church's hierarchical structure

3) the principle of collegiality.

38) How will the mass media influence the spread of the extraordinary charisms?

Much has already happened as the news of the Catholic Pentecostal Renewal spreads throughout the world. With the news media making the whole world aware of every happening, the extraordinary gifts in one part of Christ's Body will soon be known in every part.

39) Is the mass media coverage an adequate instrument for spreading the charisms?

The mass media can awaken people. The charisms themselves flourish only in a Christian community. As the print and electronic media awaken people, charismatic groups must exist to make these gifts available.

40) How will the hierarchical structure favor their spread?

This Catholic structure decides what enters into and flourishes in the Church's mainstream. The hierarchy watches over what is taught to all the nations. As the bishops see the value, possibility and power of these charisms, they will emphasize their role.

41) Why is collegiality necessary for the flourishing of charisms?

The Spirit acts according to the culture. His actions require a response fitting to the situation. The charisms are not at all monolithic. They demand flexibility and adaptation.

Collegiality allows the local Church to respond to the Spirit as He is acting within that particular community. Collegiality, adopted by Vatican II, prepares the Church's structure for a full receiving of charisms.

42) Hasn't the Pentecostal Renewal already had mass media exposure and acceptance by the hierarachy?

Strange as it might seem, God is still doing a "hidden work" within the Pentecostal Renewal. Many people know little about charisms and this Renewal. God has not as yet displayed His works, nor what can be accomplished by the charisms.

Ephesians, (Chapter 4) prophesies the victory of the Risen Christ and His goal for the whole church. "He who descended is the very one who ascended high above the heavens, that he might fill all men with His gifts." (V 10).

Chapter 14
THE POWER OF PRAYER TONGUES

Given as a sign of the Spirit's coming (Acts 2:4), as a clear signal from God that the Gentiles should be baptized (Acts 10:46), and as proof that the Baptism of Jesus was greater than the Baptism of John (Acts 19:6), prayer in tongues highlights the important moments in Early Church history.

This gift's great power is still unknown, hidden and dormant for millions of believers. These have received Jesus' Baptism but not all the powers which accompany the Spirit's presence. They have not been told about prayer tongues. They associate the gift with the Pentecostal Renewal and fail to see themselves praying in this way.

In fact, American Catholic parishes have a unique phenomenon. Those parish members who share in this Renewal understand and use prayer tongues. The parish itself knows and cares little about the gift.

The previous volume (Chapter Four) explained prayer tongues, the scriptural basis for the gift and how it is yielded to. The usual objections and problems were addressed.

None of that material will be touched on here. This chapter centers on the power of the gift, what it has done for thousands, and how important is its universal spread.

Before beginning, one explanation is needed. Prayer tongues is an abiding gift. Once the believer receives this power, he/she can pray in tongues at any moment and in any occasion. The gift seems to be available to everyone. Prayer tongues allows everyone at any time "to pray in the Spirit." The claims made for its power rest upon a daily and constant use of this never-ending manifestation.

(A)   PURPOSES OF PRAYER TONGUES

1)   *What is the purpose of prayer tongues?*

Through this gift the person:

1) praises God.

2) experiences the Spirit.

3) yields to charisms.

4) enjoys the Spirit's actions.

(B)   PRAISING GOD

2)   *How does a person praise God?*

The gift itself is praise. Peter heard the Gentiles "speaking in tongues and glorifying God." (Acts 10:46) Paul states clearly "A man who speaks in a tongue is talking not to men but to God." (1 Cor. 14:2) The usual words in tongues are praise.

3) Does this gift foster praise in the vernacular?

Using prayer tongues daily impresses upon the believer that prayer is primarily adoration of God. Praying in tongues brings about a constant attitude of praising God.

4) Don't other people, without this gift, praise God?

Most people don't give much thought to praising God. Praise does not seem like a traditional prayer. Prayer of thanksgiving or petition seem to make more sense.

Prayer tongues changes that outlook. Through this gift praising God comes easily to a large number. Prayer tongues provide a needed freedom from rational constraints which limit spontaneity in approaching God and restrict the prayer of praise.

5) How are these rational restraints overcome?

Prayer tongues, unlike natural speech or even rational prayer, bypass the person's intellect. The intellectual aspects of the prayer (the words) are supplied by the Spirit. As a result, people on a wide scale are quickly introduced to a prayer that goes beyond petition or thanksgiving.

(C) EXPERIENCING THE SPIRIT

6) How does the person experience the Spirit through this gift?

The praise words spoken in tongues open the person's rational and inner faculties to the Spirit's other actions.

7) How does this happen?

Since prayer tongues does not involve the intellect, that faculty is free to be touched directly by the Spirit. The Spirit brings thoughts to the intellect, either reminding the person from his own memory or bringing forth new thoughts within.

By praying in tongues, the believer cooperates with God's primary action. Through that prayer, the Spirit touches all the inner faculties. People experience the Spirit in their memory, imagination and feelings.

8) Does Scripture speak of this common action between the Spirit and the believer?

1) Paul directly connects prayer tongues and the praying with the mind:

> "What is my point here? I want to pray with my spirit and also with my mind. I want to sing with my spirit and with my mind as well." (1 Cor. 14:15)

2) Jesus says that the Spirit:

> "will instruct you in everything,
> and remind you of all that I told you." (Jn. 14:26)
> and
> "will guide you to all truth." (Jn. 16:13)

3) Paul writes of the common action of Holy Spirit with the human spirit:

"The Spirit himself gives witness with our spirit that we are children of God." (Rom. 8:16)

Scripture foresees a common and close working together between the Spirit and the believer.

9) What is the role of prayer tongues?

Prayer tongues initiates this common action. Tongues themselves are an action of both the Spirit and the person. Through their continued use the Spirit's activity continues and deepens.

10) Can't the Spirit's activity take place without prayer tongues?

The Spirit is not limited by any method. However, prayer tongues is the unique means to widescale and universal experiences.

D) YIELDING TO CHARISMS

11) What is the relationship of prayer tongues to charisms?

Besides religious experiences, the Spirit also gives charisms (gifts of service) for others. The same relationship occurs between prayer tongues and these charisms. When prayer tongues are used charisms abound. When prayer tongues are unknown or deliberately set aside, these charismatic manifestations fade away.

12) Does the New Testament link charisms and prayer tongues?

There is a unique joining of the two throughout the New Testament:

1) At Pentecost, besides prayers in tongues, the disciples "make bold proclamation as the Spirit prompted them." (Acts 2:4)

2) At Ephesus, the twelve disciples, besides praying in tongues, began "to utter prophecies." (Acts 19:6)

3) In 1 Cor. C. 14, Paul describes abundant charismatic activity, all intertwined with prayer in tongues.

13) Do the tongues themselves ever become charisms?

Usually the prayer tongue is a word of praise and as such does not directly serve others. However, the tongue can and frequently does change from the usual prayer of praise into a ministry tongue. With this change some charism is being used.

14) Does this phenomenon occur often?

The Spirit's charismatic actions should increase. Fidelity to prayer tongues and growth in charisms brings the person to a point where these ministry tongues are extremely frequent.

15) *What ministry tongues are frequent?*

Our own experiences highlight four ministry tongues, although others certainly exist:

1) Healing.

2) Emotional restoration.

3) Prophecy.

4) Deliverance.

E) THE SPIRIT'S ACTIONS

16) *What happens under the influence of prayer tongues?*

As the person uses this gift faithfully, all of the Spirit's actions described in the New Testament are experienced. Jesus' promise that He would send a Consoler is seen as truly fulfilled.

17) *What spiritual benefits come to the person praying in tongues?*

Those regularly using prayer tongues attest to the following:

1) a greater ease in talking personally to God.

2) a setting free from emotional bondage.

3) an ability to set problems aside.

4) greater openness to God's enlightenment.

5) clear guidance in decisions.

6) power over confusion, both internal and external.

7) a desire for the sacraments.

The list is endless. Prayer tongues releases the Spirit, and gives Him full permission to act freely. Experiencing prayer tongues and all the spiritual helps that accompany that gift show why it was better that Jesus go and send the Paraclete. (Jn. 16:7)

18) What if prayer tongues are unknown or set aside?

The Spirit continues to do these actions but the human cooperation and receptivity is limited. With that limitation the Spirit's work within is also limited.

19) Why are prayer tongues so stressed?

Prayer tongues allows the Spirit to actually do the tasks which Scripture says He is supposed to be doing. Experientially, thousands of people witness that the Spirit actually does these works within them as they began to pray in tongues.

F) PRAYER TONGUES AND THE CHURCH

20) Why has this gift of prayer tongues not been actively present in the Catholic Church before this Pentecostal Renewal?

That is a great mystery. The past reasons or causes are not very important. Using the present opportunity to restore tongues is.

21) If all the claims concerning prayer tongues are true, why don't more Catholics pray in tongues?

They don't pray in tongues because this power is not preached in our churches. Whenever praying in tongues is taught, believed in and sought, the Spirit abundantly pours forth the gift. The Spirit has no restraint. We are the ones restraining His actions.

22) Would Catholics accept this teaching?

Certainly this teaching would seem strange and new. However, Catholics would probably go through the same steps as newcomers to a prayer meeting.

At first, newcomers have fear and hesitancy. They then gain understanding and acceptance. As all Catholics became open to the gift, praying in tongues would become widespread and effective.

23) What would happen then?

A number of important results would emerge:

1) Praise of God would increase in our churches.

2) People would pray more effectively.

3) They would experience the Spirit's inner actions.

4) They would serve the Church by their charisms.

The Spirit of the New Testament would once more be seen and experienced for what He is, Jesus' final and greatest gift.

24) What if praying in tongues does not become more widespread?

The Spirit will remain hidden. Charisms will not flourish. People will be overcome by the growing powers of evil. The many spiritual and human collapses will continue.

25) Are prayer tongues that important?

Of themselves they are not. As the door to the Spirit's full powers within the person and within the Church they are.

Chapter 15
LEARNING FROM THE PENTECOSTAL CHURCHES

Originally, a small group of Catholics at Duquesne University prayed with a Pentecostal group and learned about the Baptism of the Spirit and charisms. God used that personal knowledge to spark the Catholic Pentecostal Renewal.

We still have much to learn from the Pentecostal churches. Baptism of the Spirit and charisms cannot just be added on to Church life. The Spirit is not an addition to the Catholic Church. He is the soul of the Mystical body.

The Pentecostal Churches although lacking many Catholic powers, continue to gain membership in every part of the world, including Catholic countries. What is the secret of their success? Why do they make inroads? What can we learn from them?

Before moving into the questions a certain understanding must be established:

1) The Pentecostal Churches lack many gifts that are present in the Catholic Church.

2) The Pentecostal Churches have great difficulty preserving unity among themselves.

3) This chapter does not urge the Catholic Church to become a world-wide Pentecostal Church.

This chapter has one focus, the need to continue to learn from the Pentecostal Churches.

(A)   UNDERSTANDING THE PENTECOSTAL CHURCHES

1)   What are Pentecostal churches?

These churches use the powers associated with the original Pentecost as the center and core of the Church's belief and practice. They stress the Baptism of the Spirit, praying in tongues and charisms as the primary actions within believers.

Over the years, these Pentecostal churches have assumed a variety of names, practices, doctrines and structure. Some even seem to have set aside prayer tongues, yet, the central focus on the Spirit acting within the believer remains.

2)   How do they foster personal growth?

The beginning religious experience is strengthened by a constant emphasis on personal, internal experiences. They stress the personal reading of the bible and the formation of a scriptural mentality.

3) *How do they increase the numbers who attend?*

They urge their members to witness to others, to use various means of outreach and to adapt to the local situation. They stress the importance of every believer knowing the Holy Spirit and yielding to His actions.

(B) COMPARING THE CHURCHES

4) *How would this contrast with the Catholic Church's approach?*

The Catholic Church emphasizes liturgy and sacraments. The Holy Spirit is present and acknowledged but His personal activity within the believer is not the primary focus.

5) *Is this approach better or worse than the other churches?*

This Catholic approach has some advantages and some disadvantages.

6) *What are the advantages of the Catholic approach?*

On the favorable side are the following:

1) With the stress on liturgy, a heavy demand is not placed upon the personal gifts of the priest. Therefore, every mass benefits the people independent of the priest's charisms.

2) This objective liturgy can appeal to many personality types. Church worship does not depend on the personality of the priest and offers a communal celebration open to many needs.

3   The liturgy is not overly long and can appeal to people who are only minimally religious.

7) *What are the disadvantages?*

On the negative side are the following:

1)   The pre-formed liturgy limits the charismatic activity of the priest and the people.

2)   A liturgy that becomes only a ritual exercises little influence over the daily life of the believer.

8) *Does not the Church have various parish activities, such as prayer groups, bible studies, etc. to foster these personal experiences?*

The Catholic Church has these parish activities but they are seen as secondary and optional.

This is the main difference between the Catholic and the Pentecostal Churches. The latter see religious experiences and personal conversion as central elements of Church worship. These Churches don't push these goals off to another night.

C)   THE PENTECOSTAL APPROACH

9) *Do the Pentecostal Churches merely center on the Sunday worship?*

No. The Sunday worship, the Pentecostal Church's theology (simple as it might be) and the daily life of the believer all fit together.

10) What is meant by "fitting together"?

"Fitting together" means that the Spirit's activity is central to every part of the Church's life. From that basic understanding they fashion their Sunday service, establish their goals and carry out their pastoral care.

11) Why is this important?

A clear connection exists between the Pentecostal worship and the rest of the week. The worship is not removed from daily life but overflows into the life of the believer.

12) What is a concrete example of this overflowing?

These Churches want their members to read the Bible daily. The members bring their bibles to Church and during the service the Bible is used by all. Simple as it may sound, this method is effective. The people do something at Sunday worship which they are asked to do during the week.

13) How does their worship affect the rest of the week?

These churches preach the Spirit's acitivity within the person. During the Sunday worship, the people experience the Spirit working within them. They are then encouraged to experience the Spirit acting within them during the week.

14) Is there any other goal that can be followed through on during the week?

These churches stress witnessing, telling others about the power of Jesus Christ to change a believer's life. Members of these churches use this power of witnessing on many occasions during the week. This attracts new members.

15) What then is the secret of these Churches' growth?

They have grown because their members are active. They have awakened people to spiritual activity, both in their personal religious experiences and in their witnessing to others. Members serve the church through tithing and offering of services. Many times their witnessing takes place in the context of social action.

D) THE CATHOLIC APPROACH

16) How does this contrast with the Catholic Church's approach?

The Church's theology centers on the sacraments as the important spiritual encounters with Christ. The Church's worship centers on a ritual, the Roman liturgy. The Church's pastoral practices center on preparing people for sacraments and urging them to a strong sacramental life.

17) Is this approach better or worse than the Pentecostal practices?

There are certain strengths to the Catholic approach. By stressing hierarchy and sacraments, unity is maintained. Ritual liturgy has a universal appeal. Sacraments provide an objective approach to God. The Church has unity, clarity and universality in its approach. However, it also has passivity.

18) What causes this passivity?

The Church stresses what is already existing, namely sacraments and a prayer form that is already worked out, namely liturgy. Catholics think their main goals are to attend liturgies and to receive sacraments. Both liturgy and sacraments require only a very passive participation.

19) *What is lacking?*

The average Catholic is not asked nor taught how to be active, either in the Church's worship, in his own prayer life, in witnessing to others, or in the Church's missionary activity.

20) *Is not this the "age of the laity" and have not many more lay people become active in the Catholic Church?*

Yes, but the lay people are usually just doing what the formerly more numerous priests and religious used to do. There has been no widescale enlarging of the Church's goals.

(E) THE CURSILLO MOVEMENT

21) *Did not the "Cursillo Movement" embody some of the goals of the Pentecostal Churches?*

Yes, the goals of the Cursillo Movement were a personal relationship to God and service to the Church.

22) *Why is the Cursillo Movement no longer a powerful force in the Catholic Church?*

Within the Church, every movement either becomes part of the church's life or it fades away. A movement has its special time. The gift is either incorporated into the Church or it is lost.

23) How does this incorporation happen?

It can happen in two basic ways.

1) The movement can become a religious order. Thus the poverty movement of St. Francis of Assisi or the preaching movement of St. Dominic remain in the Church through their communities.

2) The goals of the Movement are permanently incorporated into the very mainstream of the Church. This has happened to the Liturgical Movement at Vatican II.

(F) THE PENTECOSTAL RENEWAL OF CATHOLICISM

24) Should the Catholic Church become a Pentecostal Church?

No. If it did, the Church would lose many important gifts that God has given to the Church. The Pentecostal focus on personal religious experiences is too narrow and divisive.

25) What should the Church become?

The Church should become a Pentecostally renewed Church, whereby the Pentecostal gifts share the importance now placed on liturgy and sacraments.

26) Wouldn't the Catholic Church then look and act like a Pentecostal Church?

There is no need to look and act like any Pentecostal Church. There would be the bringing forth of a new reality, which borrows the power and enthusiasm of these new Churches while preserving the 2000 years of wisdom.

27) Have we not already borrowed enough from these Pentecostal Churches in allowing the Catholic Pentecostal Renewal to exist?

We have borrowed from these churches but we haven't totally learned from them. Their continued growth, especially in areas which were formerly Catholic strongholds, reminds us that we have a long way to go to see a New Pentecost in our day.

28) Does not the Catholic Church have traditions while those churches lack the centuries of tradition?

Tradition is both a help and a hindrance. The Catholic tradition has held on to the essential truths and has the wisdom of experience.

However, Churches without such a tradition can be more in contact with the present situation. They are freer to adapt their worship and pastoral practices to the people. They seem to take advantage of the mass media. They stress personal initiative, not waiting for church authorities to authorize ministries.

The churches without long traditions make many mistakes. However, they also do many things that bring Jesus Christ into the modern world. Without doubt, these new churches are having a tremendous impact, as witnessed by their growth and popularity.

29)   What is the role of the Catholic Pentecostal Renewal?

More than any other sector of the Catholic Church this Renewal understands the dynamic force of the Pentecostal Churches. Through this Renewal Catholics do become active and learn how to pray and to witness. This Renewal has borrowed the Pentecostal powers and developed some of its own traditions.

30)   What is missing?

These Pentecostal powers are not interacting with all the varied aspects of Roman Catholicism. This Renewal is compartmentalized, and sealed in, so to speak, in prayer groups and prayer communities. How Pentecostalism can renew the Church is still unanswered because it has not yet been tried by the whole Church.

31)   What could the bishops do?

The bishops could:

1)   examine all the powers, practices, theology and working of the Pentecostal Churches.

2)   see which parts should be introduced into the Catholic Church.

3)   require the changes that should take place.

In other words the bishops should take a page out of their book and slip it into ours.

Section Four
Special Issues

CHAPTER 16
MARY AND THE
RENEWAL

Some Catholics complain that Mary is left out of this Renewal. Other Catholics remove her entirely because of ecumenism. Most Catholics don't grasp her relation to the Spirit and are not even clear about the Church's teaching on Mary.

This chapter is not an extra, thrown in because something should be written about Mary. Her role is too intertwined with the Spirit to be considered "an extra". She says that "God who is mighty has done great things for me." (Lk 1:49) and has prophesied (in the inspired words of scripture) that "all ages to come shall call me blessed." (1:48)

She is present at all the important moments. When the Spirit begets Jesus, she is there. When Jesus works his first miracle, she is there. When Jesus dies, she is there. When Jesus sends His Spirit, she is there. How could she always be so present in God's plan, and yet not be part of our idea of coming to God?

A correct doctrinal basis is needed. After that, this chapter can move into the practical questions surrounding Mary and the Renewal. (Written on the Feast of Our Lady of Mount Carmel, July 16, 1985)

(A) BASIC CATHOLIC BELIEFS

1) *What do Catholics believe about Mary?*

Catholics believe the following:

a) *As Mother*

1) She is the true physical mother of Jesus.

2) Being the mother of Jesus, she is correctly called the mother of God.

3) Mary conceived Jesus by the Holy Spirit overshadowing her.

b) *Personal privileges*

4) The Holy Spirit possessed her soul from the first moment of her conception.

5) Mary never committed any personal sin.

6) Mary, body and soul, was assumed into heaven.

c) *Role in the Church*

7) Mary is the pre-eminent member of the Communion of Saints.

8) Mary is the Mediatrix of all graces.

9) Mary is mother of the Church.

(B) PRIVILEGES AS MOTHER

2) When and why did the Church define that Mary is the Mother of God?

This teaching was defined by the Council of Ephesus (431). At that time, the question was whether Jesus Christ was one person or two persons. (The Church teaches that Jesus Christ has two complete natures, human and divine, but is only one person, the Second Person of the Trinity).

If Jesus were two persons, human and divine, then Mary could not be the mother of God but only mother of the human person. Defining Mary as "mother of God" was the easiest and clearest way for the Church to say that Jesus Christ, although having two natures, was only one person.

3) When did the Church define that Mary virginally conceived Jesus by the action of the Spirit?

Since this belief is based on the gospel accounts of Matthew (1:18-25) and Luke (1:26-38), the virginal conception was believed from the beginning.

This doctrine was officially defined in the Creed of Constantinople (381) and after that has regularly been a part of various Church creeds.

4) Does Catholic teaching go beyond the virginal conception?

The Catholic doctrine of Mary's virginity has two other parts:

1) God preserved Mary's virginity even in giving birth.

2)   After the birth, Mary lived as the virgin spouse of Joseph.

5)   Why do Catholics so stress this virgin birth concept?

The virgin birth highlights that Jesus Christ's coming is the beginning of the new age of a redeemed humanity.

The Spirit's role in Jesus' conception represents the constant progress in the Early Church's thinking about the relationship of Jesus to the Spirit. Eventually, John's gospel will clearly place that relationship as existing even before conception, since "In the beginning was the Word." (1:1)

(C)   PERSONAL PRIVILEGES

6)   What is meant by the Immaculate Conception?

It means that the Holy Spirit dwelt in and totally possessed Mary's soul from the first moment of her own conception. Since every other human being inherits a human nature tainted by original sin, this Spirit's action in Mary is called the Immaculate Conception.

7)   How could Mary's freedom from sin result from Christ's redeeming death which took place many years later?

Mary's freedom from sin resulted from an outpouring of the Spirit into her soul. Theologians see every Spirit outpouring as resulting from the death and resurrection of Jesus. Since God is not limited by time, Mary's freedom from sin came from the foreseen merits of her Son.

8) How was the Church led to define the Immaculate Conception?

The New Testament (Matt. Chap 1 and Luke Chap 2) pictures Mary as a holy woman. The Church, after defining Mary as the mother of God, saw that her holiness was flawless from the very beginning. The doctrine of the Immaculate Conception was defined in 1854 by Pope Pius IX.

9) What happened after that papal declaration?

Shortly afterward, Mary appeared at Lourdes, France, telling Bernadette that she was the Immaculate Conception. The young girl was totally unaware of the doctrine or its recent definition.

10) Can it be proven that Mary never committed any sin?

No strict proof can be given. However, a clear explanation explaining the doctrine is possible.

Mary needed Christ's redemptive death as much as any human being. This doctrine of Mary's sinlessness merely recognizes that Jesus' work in her was total, complete and before the fact. God's work in preserving Mary from sin prepared for His even greater work, the overshadowing by the Spirit in conceiving Jesus.

11) What is meant by Mary's Assumption?

The exact words of Pius XII's definition are that Mary "having completed the course of her earthly life was assumed, body and soul, into heavenly glory."

The Apostles' Creed teaches that everyone will rise, body and soul. This doctrine means that Mary enjoys now what every saved person will someday experience. Again, God does earlier for Mary, what He wants to do for everyone.

12) How do Catholics understand the Communion of Saints?

The Communion of Saints, also taught clearly in the Apostles' Creed, means that all the saved, besides enjoying union with Christ, are also united to each other in spiritual sharing and help.

13) Why is Mary the preeminent member of the Communion of Saints?

Each one's role in the Body of Christ is determined by God's will. "Just as each of us has one body with many members, and not all members have the same function, so too we, though many, are one body in Christ and individually members one of another. We have gifts that differ according to the favor bestowed on each of us". (Rom. 12:4-6) Since Mary's gift was to be God's mother and because of her total cooperation with the Spirit, she is seen by Catholics as the preeminent member of the Communion of Saints.

14) Why does Mary's role as intercessor pertain to every member of Christ's body?

Before accepting Mary's role, the believer must accept the more basic truth that a spiritual interaction of mutual help takes place among Christ's members. (If fallen angels can keep us away from Christ, why cannot members of Christ's body help us to be one with Him?).

If that basic belief is accepted, then Mary's role becomes clear. She is a helping member of the Communion of Saints. Since Jesus is the head of the Body, Mary, as His Mother, extends her helping role to everyone.

(D)   MARY AND SCRIPTURE

15)   Is not Mary very much in the backgound of Jesus' public life?

In the first three gospels, Mary appears just once during Jesus' public life (Mt. 12:46-50; Mk 3:31-35; and Lk. 8:19-21). In this one instance, Jesus deliberately rejects any claim upon Him due to this physical relationship. He asks "Who is my mother? Who are my brothers?" (Mt. 12:48).

Two explanations are given for Jesus' repudiation of any special claim of Mary:

1)   Mary accepted the usual role of Jewish women who were not in the public limelight.

2)   The rebuke stressed the greater importance of a spiritual relationship to Jesus rather than a physical one. The Early Church had many physical relatives of Jesus. The rebuke removed any claim these might have to a Church role based on their physical relationship to Jesus.

16) What does the Catholic Church use as the scriptural basis for devotion to Mary?

That basis is:

1) the infancy narratives of Mathew and Luke.

2) John's gospel stressing Mary as mother.

3) the specific mention of Mary's presence at Pentecost. (Acts 1:14)

17) Why is Mary's scriptural role so large in the infancy narrative?

The early Church progressed in understanding Jesus' relationship to the Spirit.

1) In the beginning, they saw that Jesus enjoyed the Spirit after His Resurrection.

2) They then realized that Jesus must have received the Spirit at the beginning of His ministry. The signs of His baptism proclaim the union of Jesus and the Spirit.

3) Next, they realized that Jesus' union with the Spirit was from the first moment of His conception, a truth brought out by Mary's role in the infancy narratives.

4) Finally, in John's gospel, the Church realizes that Jesus' relationship to the Spirit existed even before His conception. Mary becomes more prominent as the Church better understands the relationship of Jesus to the Holy Spirit.

18) Why is Mary more prominent in John?

At Cana, John four times identifies Mary as the mother of Jesus. (2:1,3,5 and 12). At the cross, he doesn't even use her name but says "Near the cross of Jesus there stood his mother". (19:25)

To John, her name was not as important as her role. She is the mother of Jesus through whom the Word was made flesh.

(E) MEDIATRIX OF ALL GRACES

19) What do Catholics mean in calling Mary "The Mediatrix of all Graces"?

This title refers to two activities of Mary:

1) Her role in life in the redemptive death of Jesus.

2) Her role now in interceding for God's graces.

20) What was Mary's role in Jesus' life?

Her physical role in Christ's death is clear from the gospel which describes her as standing at the Cross. (Jn. 19:20). What Jesus shared with her from His foreknowledge about His crucifixion is not clear. Certainly she shared in God's Redemptive plan. (What would have happened if she refused God's request to be His mother?)

21) What does the Church teach about Mary's intercession?

The Church teaches that all of God's graces involve Our Lady's intercession whether the person invokes Mary or not. This teaching is rooted in Mary's sharing in Christ's redemptive work.

22) For Catholics, what is safe to believe?

It is safe for Catholics to say that Mary cooperated in Christ's redemptive act and that she continues this role in the Communion of Saints.

23) Why does Mary enjoy such a prominent role in granting favors?

First, much sound theology provides a basis for her role.

Secondly, and perhaps more to the point, Marian devotions kept alive the charismatic gifts. In a time when the Spirit was hidden, Marian devotions openly sought divine interventions.

24) Did Mary supplant the Holy Spirit?

Catholics never believed that Mary supplanted the Holy Spirit. However, the Catholic belief in charisms was most prominent in the Marian devotions.

Healings and other charisms were associated with Lourdes and Fatima, and favors to petitions (often extraordinary) surrounded the Miraculous Medal Novena.

25) Must a person know that Mary is the Mediatrix of all Graces?

Neither knowing her role nor invoking Mary is necessary. However, knowing God's plan increases the human cooperation. Knowing that Jesus is the Mediator between God and man helps us to the Father. Understanding the Communion of Saints (which includes Mary) is another help.

(F)   MARY AND THE PENTECOSTAL RENEWAL

26) Should Marian devotions be introduced into the Prayer Meeting?

Prayer meetings are modeled after 1 Cor. C14 and focus on the Spirit's charisms. Marian devotions tend to have quite a different focus. Trying to have both together doesn't seem appropriate.

27) Why isn't Mary stressed more at prayer meetings?

Many aspects of Catholic life aren't stressed at a prayer meeting. The meeting focuses on proclaiming Jesus as Lord and yielding to charisms. As long as all is done in order, no one can accuse the leaders of not stressing Mary.

28) Shouldn't the rosary be recited at a prayer meeting?

Catholics should pray the rosary daily and at times, should gather to pray the rosary communally.

However, saying the rosary is a different communal prayer than the prayer meeting. The prayer meeting has the goal of praising God by means of charisms given by the Spirit.

29) Are any prayers to Mary appropriate at a prayer meeting?

A prayer meeting should not be turned into a Marian devotion. However, the other extreme also has to be avoided. Since the Catholic Church teaches and fosters devotion to Mary, some expressions of this devotion are certainly appropriate at a Catholic Pentecostal prayer meeting.

30) What is Mary's role in the Renewal?

1) A Catholic involved in the Renewal should know the Church's teaching on Mary.

2) The person, and the prayer group, should enter into Marian feasts contained in the Church's liturgical year.

3) The person should often use Mary's Magnificat (Lk. 1:46:55) as a prayer model.

31) What about private devotions to Mary?

These devotions, such as the rosary, are traditional and have a long history in the Church. People should be encouraged to pray the rosary daily.

(G)   MARY AND THE SPIRIT

32)   *Why should charismatics have devotion to Mary?*

The New Testament narrates two sendings of the Spirit.

By the first sending, the Spirit formed the physical body of Jesus Christ. "The Holy Spirit will come upon you and the power of the Most High will overshadow you; hence, the holy offspring to be born will be called Son of God." (Lk. 1:35)

In the second sending, (on Pentecost) the Spirit formed the Mystical Body of Christ "You, then are the body of Christ." (1 Cor. 12:27)

Only Mary was present on both occasions. Those interested in the sending of the Spirit should have special devotion to Mary. She is always where the Spirit is.

33)   **Doesn't devotion to Mary detract from devotion to the Holy Spirit?**

1)   In the years when the Holy Spirit (then called the "Holy Ghost") was very much the hidden or forgotten Person, Catholics were very open to His actions through the Marian devotions.

2)   When Catholic Pentecostals began to preach about healings, Marian shrines were cited.

3)   A number of saints, centuries ago, prophecised a tremendous age of the Spirit. They always linked this Age of the Spirit to Marian devotions.

34) Why is Mary so linked to the Spirit?

The Holy Spirit Himself never assumed a human nature. He uses our human natures for His manifestations. "To each person the manifestation of the Spirit is given for the common good." (1 Cor 12:7) Mary allowed the Holy Spirit to totally use her human nature to form Christ's human nature.

Luke in his gospel and in the Acts, deliberately forges similarities between the Annunciation scene and Jesus' promise of Pentecost:

"The Holy Spirit will come upon you." (Lk. 1:35)

"...when the Holy Spirit comes down on you." (Acts 1:8)

and

"...the power of the Most High will overshadow you." (Lk. 1:35)

"You will receive power..." (Acts 1:8)

Mary, totally submitting to the Spirit, teaches everyone to yield to charisms.

35) Why is Mary important to this Renewal?

The Lord, and no one else, builds this house. All must respect His plan.

Since God has so clearly included Mary in His plans, those who arbitrarily remove her are closing themselves off to some aspect of God's will.

36) *What is Mary's special prerogative as Mother of the Church?*

Mary is closely linked with the Church. In Revelations, the woman successfully conceives and gives birth. (12:13) That woman is the New Israel, the Church, brought about by the Spirit's sending. Mary, the woman, always associated with the Spirit and the Church, shows where victory and not defeat, can be gained. Victory is with Jesus who was "born of a woman." (Gal. 4:4)

Chapter 17
GOD'S HIDDEN DESIGNS

Outsiders view charismatics as people who wildly raise their arms, try to pray in unintelligible syllables and constantly claim divine interventions and visions. If the charismatics are thoughtful, kind and balanced, then a certain toleration enters in. People willingly admit, "even some of my best friends are charismatics." Many wish the movement would just go away and that the charismatics would finally see that much of the so-called phenomenon is really due to mass emotionalism or hysteria.

Those feelings are natural ones for the outsider. Hearing claims of God's actions and not sharing in them generates confused feelings. The person feels more comfortable with parish life where there are relatively few divine phenomena. Parish worship centers on a sacramental life which all can easily share no matter what their own personal religious involvement.

Does God want Catholics to feel uncomfortable? Are the negative feelings really a beginning step? Why does this Renewal generate so many feelings on every side? What are God's hidden designs for a Renewal that began so suddenly, grew so rapidly and has manifested so many divine signs? This chapter talks about God's hidden designs. The claims are not made from human strengths but from the total inability of this Renewal to effect any change unless God intervenes directly and powerfully.

(A) GOD'S INITIATIVE

1) What are the strengths of this Renewal?

Some come directly from God. Others have resulted from the years of cooperation with the Spirit's actions.

2) What comes from God?

1) God founded this Renewal. Therefore the Renewal itself claims no human founders. The 1967 events which began this Renewal, were so obviously God's own intervention that only God is seen as the founder. This contrasts with other Renewals which usually began from human founders.

2) God supplies the gifts of religious experiences and charisms. No one else can bestow prayer tongues or prayer experiences or any of the charisms.

3) God gives the on-going direction. Plans for events or decisions for the Renewal's direction are given to leaders through prophecy or other charisms.

God, then, began this Renewal, provides the religious experiences and should personally guide the whole operation. Where there has been true failure or collapse, the leaders were using their own powers and going in their own direction.

3) *What comes from human cooperation?*

Just as the clay molded by the potter becomes capable of service, so human beings formed by God's action have some personal strengths. The following are the most essential:

1) A beginning knowledge of the extent of God's actions.

2) A greater faith in divine intervention.

3) An understanding of God's call.

4) Awareness of the door to religious experiences.

5) Power to live in the Spirit.

6) Wisdom needed to foster the Spirit's actions.

All of those strengths are totally dependent on God's on-going initiatives.

(B) UNDERSTANDING GOD'S ACTIONS

4) *Why is it important to see that God Himself started this Renewal?*

God initiates every true renewal within the Church. Therefore, the uniqueness is not God's initiative, but God's *direct* initiative. God constantly initiates gifts for the Church, but usually through a definite founder (as with religious communities). His continued action is within the founder's original charisms.

This Renewal has no founder and no such limitation exists. This Renewal doesn't focus on the charism of poverty (as

St. Francis of Assisi) or of preaching (as St. Dominic) or on any particular charism. This Renewal focuses on all the charisms. Since God is the founder, every action of the Spirit is part of this Renewal.

5) Isn't the Spirit active in many believers who don't belong to this Renewal?

Hopefully, the Spirit is acting upon all believers, inside or outside of this Renewal. That doesn't lessen God's designs in any way.

6) If the Spirit is working everywhere, then why is this Renewal so important?

Hopefully, an analogy will explain. God was working upon all mankind, before He sent Jesus. The Word becoming flesh was the Father's direct initiative to bring His universal work to fulfillment. Even though people already were experiencing God's actions, Jesus was not superfluous.

So, people already experienced the Spirit before this Renewal began. The Renewal is God's direct initiative. In God's design, this Renewal also, is not superfluous.

7) How does the analogy of Jesus apply to this Renewal?

Remembering that it is an analogy, allows the following comparison to be made.

Many people who never heard of Jesus have been saved by God's work within them. Hearing about and believing in Jesus heightens, strengthens, guides and protects God's work.

Many who have never heard of this Renewal experience the Holy Spirit. Hearing about and participating in the Renewal, confirms, strengthens and solidifies the Spirit's work.

(C)   THE SPIRIT AND THE RENEWAL

8)   Why does the Spirit need this Renewal to be effective?

This Renewal claims no monopoly on the Spirit who is active always and everywhere. However, His actions can be limited by lack of human understanding, cooperation and perseverance.

God, who so much wants this to be an age of the Spirit, initiated this Renewal so the Spirit's work in all mankind is not frustrated by human failures.

9)   How can someone who is experiencing the Spirit need this Renewal?

Every person has the power to read, yet all need schools to develop that gift. Internal actions of the Spirit are not enough. People need an external help so these inner actions are fully developed.

10)   What, then, is God's design?

From God's own design, this Renewal focuses on every personal experience of the Spirit. In whatever way the Spirit acts or wants to act within people, He can use this Renewal as His instrument.

Since the Renewal's focus is the Spirit Himself, the Renewal's scope is universal, just as Jesus is the universal way to God.

11) How is God's design revealed by the Renewal's confidence in religious experiences and charisms.

Again, these come from God. The Renewal, by itself, is helpless. If the wind of the Spirit fails to blow, the Renewal's ship moves nowhere. However, this human powerlessness is God's strength.

No human person can decide to generate true charisms. This Renewal is based upon God's decision to pour out religious experiences and charisms. As such, it is an awakening to what God is doing daily in our midst.

12) How does God's daily guidance reveal His design?

God is not just the Founder of this Renewal and source of its charisms. He is also the One who truly guides this Renewal.

Again, this goes back to God as Founder. A human founder does not just begin a movement but also guides the process and provides instructions for its continued growth.

Every human founder is limited. God is not. God's beginning action and His continuing guidance are the same. He enlightens people concerning His will and provides needed directions. To receive directions from God requires charismatic activity, the very heart of this Renewal.

Other movements don't need God's direct guidance as much as this Renewal. God, who provides on-going guidance by His charisms, hints that He has special designs.

(D)   A SCRIPTURAL MODEL

13)   Is the Renewal totally helpless?

God delights in equipping people for service. He enjoys having people learn His ways and grow confident that He will act. This is God's way as outlined in Scripture. In the Renewal, this regular biblical process is happening.

Not just God's action and our helplessness show His design. People being equipped by God for service manifests the same divine action as God displayed in biblical times. This is not surprising because the reappearance of charisms is also a renewed manifestation of scriptural powers.

14)   What in the Renewal is similar to the scriptural picture?

Like Abraham and Moses, people realize they are experiencing a unique divine intervention. Like the early Christian community, they come together to cooperate with this intervention and make it available to others.

God's actions experienced in this Renewal, are similar to both the Old and New Testament interventions.

15)   What is the importance of these communally held experiences?

Since religious experiences usually come through a believing community, this Renewal offers to the Church the possibility of universal religious experiences and the outpouring of charisms upon all mankind.

Just as a single medical discovery can help the whole world, so this Renewal contains within itself (by God's gracious design) the power to renew the face of the earth.

16) Isn't that an extraordinary claim for a Renewal Movement?

If the Renewal were founded by a human being (even someone under God's guidance) based on human powers (even aided by God) and guided by human wisdom (even enlightened by God) then such a claim would indeed be exaggerated.

However, if this Renewal is seen as founded by God, relying on God's powers and totally following God's directions, then the claim of world-wide changes is not far fetched. The Renewal's direct focusing on the Holy Spirit leads to the conclusion that its ultimate purpose is to renew the face of the earth.

17) Isn't that the task of the Church and not of any Renewal within the Church?

It will only be in and through the Church that this Renewal will accomplish God's universal plan of bringing about the Age of the Spirit.

(E) SCRIPTURAL BASIS

18) *What does Scripture say about God's saving plan?*

Scripture always sees God's greatest actions coming from God's own initiative:

a) To Abraham:

> "When Abram was ninety-nine years old, the Lord appeared to him and said: 'I am God the Almighty. Walk in my presence and be blameless. Between you and me I will establish my covenant, and I will multiply you exceedingly.' " (Gen. 17: 1 and 2)

b) To Moses:

> "Therefore I have come down to rescue them from the hands of the Egyptians and lead them out of that land." (Ex. 3:8)

c) To David:

> "The Lord said (to Samuel), 'There – anoint him, for this is he.' " (1 Sam 16:12)

d) In Jesus:

> "Praised be the God and Father of our Lord Jesus Christ, who has bestowed on us in Christ every spiritual blessing in the heavens!" (Eph. 1:3)

19) *What happens after this divine initiative?*

God always provides on-going directions:

a) To Abraham:

"Go forth from the land of your kinsfolk and from your father's house to a land that I will show you." (Gen. 12:1)

b) To Moses:

"But Moses said to God, 'Who am I that I should go to Pharoah and lead the Israelites out of Egypt?' He answered, 'I will be with you;...' " (Ex 3:11-12)

c) To David:

"I have been with you wherever you went, and I have destroyed all your enemies before you. And I will make you famous like the great ones of the earth." (2 Sam. 7:9)

d) In Jesus to the disciples:

"And know that I am with you always, until the end of the world!" (Mt. 28:20)

20) *How do these texts refer to this Renewal?*

They show that when God directly initiates an action and directly guides it to completion, that action can have permanent and world-wide effect.

If this Renewal was begun by God's direct intervention and if the Renewal is guided by God then this divine action can also have permanent and world-wide effects.

(F) THE EARLY CHURCH

21) *Did the Early Church make claims of being permanent and world-wide?*

Their claims include the following:

1) Their mission was world-wide. (Mt. 28:19)

2) Their founder, Jesus, was greater than Moses. (Heb. C3)

3) They possessed the Keys to the Kingdom. (Mt. 16:19)

4) They were the true heirs of God's promise. (Gal. 4:21-31)

5) They attained what Israel did not. (Rom. 9:30-33)

22) *What were these claims based on ?*

These claims were not based on overwhelming numbers but upon a clear recognition of God's work in their midst.

"In times past, God spoke in fragmentary and varied ways to our fathers through the prophets; in this, the final age, he has spoken to us through his Son." (Heb. 1:1-2)

23) Were these claims surprising?

Given that they were only a small band of Jews believing in Jesus and just a part of the large, world-wide synagogue system, the claims of the Early Church are astounding. Since their history went back only to Jesus (whereas the synagogue had a centuries long tradition) their idea of themselves is truly remarkable.

24) How did they see God's action?

They saw clearly that God had acted from His own initiative:

> "Yes, God so loved the world
> that he gave his only Son." (Jn. 3:16)

They also saw that God would give continued help.

> "This treasure we possess in earthen vessels to make it clear that its surpassing power comes from God and not from us." (2 Cor. 4:7)

25) What would be the scriptural picture of the Early Church?

The Early Church consisted of:

1) a relatively small group of believers.

2) who realized they possessed tremendous prerogatives.

3) because God had taken the initiative and sent His Son into their midst.

26) *How does that compare with this Renewal?*

The Renewal consists of:

1) a relatively small group.

2) which sees itself as having tremendous gifts.

3) because God has taken the initiative and stirred up the Spirit in their midst.

27) *Is this Renewal foreordained to succeed?*

Too many errors and mistakes are possible and the Renewal has no divine promise of success. However, seeing the Renewal in the light of God's initiative and continued guidance, shows the Renewal is the recipient of a special divine design.

28) *What is the importance of this Chapter?*

Ending the book with this chapter asks the reader to blank out the many human failings associated with this Renewal and to see beyond the social phenomenon to the core of the mystery. That mystery is a sudden, unexpected outpouring of the Spirit and continued divine guidance.

Paul claimed, "...I have never shrunk from announcing to you God's design in its entirety" (Acts 20:27) At this point no one knows God's entire design. There is, however, a belief in "the mysterious design which for ages was hidden in God, the Creator of all." (Eph 3:9) This "mysterious design" is being revealed in our midst.

NOTES

NOTES

NOTES

NOTES

NOTES

NOTES